REFINING YOUR LIFE

Zen Master Dōgen
& Kōshō Uchiyama

REFINING YOUR LIFE

From the Zen Kitchen to Enlightenment

translated by Thomas Wright

New York · WEATHERHILL · *Tokyo*

This volume contains translations of Zen Master Dōgen's *Tenzo Kyōkun* (Instructions for the Zen Cook), as it appears in the *Eiheigen Zenji Shingi*, an official compilation of Dōgen's works by Reiyō Endō, and of Kōshō Uchiyama Rōshi's *Jinsei Ryōri no Hon* (How to Cook Your Life), published by the Sōtō-shū Shūmuchō in 1956 and 1970 respectively.

First edition, 1983
Third printing, 1987

Published by John Weatherhill, Inc., of New York and Tokyo, with editorial offices at 7-6-13 Roppongi, Minato-ku, Tokyo 106, Japan. Protected by copyright under terms of the International Copyright Union; all rights reserved. Printed in Japan.

Library of Congress Cataloging in Publication Data: Dōgen, 1200–1253. / Refining your life. / Translation of: Tenzo kyōkun / Dōgen. / Includes Index. / 1. Monastic and religious life (Zen Buddhism) 2. Cookery—Religious aspects—Sōtō-shū. 3. Monasticism and religious orders, Zen—Rules. I. Wright, Thomas. II. Uchiyama, Kōshō, 1912– . Jinsei ryōri no hon. English. 1983. III. Title. / BQ9449.D654 T4613 1983 294.3′4448 / 82-20295 ISBN 0-8348-0179-5

Contents

Translator's Introduction

The following text of the *Tenzo Kyōkun*, or as I have entitled it in English, *Instructions for the Zen Cook*, was written over a period of years by Eihei Dōgen Zenji (1200–1253), who was intimately familiar with both the Rinzai and Sōtō schools of Zen, and finally completed in 1237. More specifically, it was written for Dōgen's immediate disciples living with him in a monastery in medieval Japan. Now what possible connection could a text written for a group of monks some 750 years ago have for present-day Europeans and Americans neither living in a monastery nor particularly familiar with a society or way of looking at life which differs totally from our modern Western societies? That is the question to which Kōshō Uchiyama Rōshi addressed himself when he began writing the commentary that accompanies Dōgen's text.

The answer to that question, of course, depends upon the universal nature of the subject that is being addressed. In other words, such a text will have no relevancy at all if the problems that Dōgen deals with concern only a small group of male Buddhist practitioners of Kamakura-period Japan (1185–1336). I have personally found that not to be the case, especially thanks to my teacher Uchiyama Rōshi who, I believe, succeeded in pulling out those portions of the text that upon first glance seem very esoteric—perhaps bewildering is a better word—and discussed the significance such passages had for him as a twentieth-century disciple of Dōgen.

As a translator, the original text and Uchiyama Rōshi's commentary presented entirely different problems. At times Dōgen Zenji's writings, just as classical literature, border on the impenetrable even for the present-day Japanese reader; much more so will they appear that way for a long time to a person not born in Japan nor educated from childhood to read Chinese characters. More than that, however, Dōgen's logic is a big problem for Western readers, not to mention translators. If readers familiar with previous translations of Dōgen were to compare versions of the same writing, they would be startled to find a copious variety of interpretations for the same passage. One reason for this is that different translators will naturally express themselves differently. Yet another, deeper reason is that a translator, though familiar with the language, may be unaware of the reality behind the words.

Here is where years of practice come in. For me, to translate any work of Dōgen's without basing my daily life upon his most fundamental teaching, that is, *jijuyū-zammai,* or zazen, would be meaningless. Unless the posture of one's life addresses the same questions Dōgen Zenji addressed, there is little hope that the translation will be much more than a technically correct but totally incomprehensible work.

The difficulty for me over the years in regard to Dōgen's logic has been how to understand the route Dōgen took from his proposition to his conclusion. Though I might have been able to follow the development of his thought, it always seemed that somewhere along the line he made a twist or bend that did not fit into the expected route of the logic of my mind. For a long time I thought that this was mostly due to the fact that Dōgen was Japanese and I am American, and that that was the way Japanese people in those days thought. More and more, however, I have come to see the arrogance of such thinking, and that the problem lay not with Dōgen's logic, but rather with the expectations I brought to the text. Besides that, it was not logic per se that Dōgen took up as his life work, but rather the very nature and complexities of the reality of our life and death.

I would never say, nor even imply, that after fourteen or fifteen years I now have a fairly good view of Dōgen Zenji's Zen. What points this out to me more than anything else is my own day-to-day life where I am constantly discovering inconsistencies and gaps of negligence. Brooding over these aspects of one's own attitude could lead one to a kind of self-browbeating or worse. Yet ignoring these things would lead to nothing but another kind of egotistical arrogance. Reflecting on them surely becomes an influence, albeit at times a very painful one, which can reveal to us the false and delusive motives of our actions. And, though "reflecting," as I am using the word here, upon some object, whatever it might be, is not the same as *shikan-taza* (just doing zazen), it is surely something that we as human beings must not lose sight of.

As to the problems Uchiyama Rōshi's commentary presents for the translator, linguistically they are almost on the opposite end of the spectrum from Dōgen Zenji's text. Despite his having graduated from Waseda University in Tokyo with a master's degree in Western philosophy, Uchiyama Rōshi's style is not that of a philosopher or scholar. It is uncomplicated, with his examples often drawn from current events in Japan or from his own life. I have asked him about this at various times over the years, and his reply is that he has chosen a style almost totally devoid of Buddhist expressions and jargon in order to reach a much wider audience not limited to Buddhist scholars and religious specialists.

Herein lies a problem, particularly for American and European readers. Precisely because his style is easy to follow there is a danger that the reader will skim over what is being said without digging deeper to take a look at the work as a whole, seeing the ramifications of the examples being used.

To point out one such example, he discusses the problem of a married man who writes to an advice column asking what he should do for he has fallen in love with a young woman working in his office. A superficial reading of this example might lead one to think that Uchiyama Rōshi merely advocates that the young man wake up from his dream and go back to the reality of taking care of his family. However, which way the man should choose is not the issue here at all. Whichever way he goes he will have problems. The deeper problem is mistaking a "fact" in life for the "truth" of life, the former simply being an aspect of our psychological or emotional landscape by which we need not be pulled and tossed about, while the latter is that reality of life upon which we settle as "true adults." "True adults" is an expression the Rōshi uses to mean bodhisattvas.

Menzan Zuihō, an early eighteenth-century disciple of Dōgen writes in *Jijuyū-zammai*: "Generally, analogies are used for making it easier to grasp something similar to reality when we are unable to show the reality directly. You should know that analogies are useful as far as they go, but that they do not show reality as a whole. For example, when you are asked what the sun is like by a person who was born blind, you might give him a metal basin to enable him to understand that the shape of the sun is round saying, 'The sun is like this.' The man may hit the basin and reply, 'Aha! The sun makes a good sound.' You have to be very careful not to misinterpret analogies or you will go astray."

In other words, we have to be careful not to stick our heads too far into the example and lose sight of the point which is being made.

Stepping back from the problem of analogies and language for a moment, here in the latter quarter of the twentieth century, half of humanity appears to be dying of starvation, while the other half appears to be choking on its own materialism, all but unaware of its own condition. I doubt that there are many people in the world who would gladly lower their standard of living, unless they felt assured that in doing so, on the whole, their life would be much better. Nor can I offer any political panacea to solve the problem. The late Kōdō Sawaki Rōshi and former teacher of Uchiyama Rōshi used to say again and again that loss is enlightenment, gain is illusion.

Is it possible to gain greater happiness, or peace of mind, or courage, or sexual power, or greater charisma by doing zazen? There are many advocates of zazen in America and Europe today (and in Japan as well) who hold out these carrots for people to bite into. But as long as there is a hope or expectation of some result to be derived from zazen, then zazen is tainted. In the same way, when any action in our day-to-day life is motivated by some expectant result, or by what only appears to be a real condition or circumstance in our life, that expectant result is very likely to be dashed to pieces.

What are clear or undefiled activities? What are the activities of true adults in the world today? That is what *Instructions for the Zen Cook* is all about. Uchiyama Rōshi subtitled his interpretive translation and commentary of this important work *Jinsei Ryōri no Hon,* or *How to Cook Your Life*. The word *ryōri,* the meaning of which to be sure includes the cooking and preparation of food, also has broader connotations. *Ryōri* may also be used in the sense of conducting or handling one's affairs. The implication of this title is that the author tells us how we should go about conducting our lives and treating everything that comes up in our lives.

I first began working on the *Tenzo Kyōkun* about nine years ago. At the time, I was told that it was an important religious text, and that it would be good if someone were to translate it for Western readers. I was also told that the *Eihei Daishingi* (Regulations for Eihei-ji Monastery), of which the *Tenzo Kyōkun* is the first chapter, was one of the easier works of Dōgen, since it deals with practical matters.

Up until that time, I had been practicing zazen for about five years at Antai-ji, a little known temple in northern Kyoto where Uchiyama Rōshi served as abbot. During those early years I had very little interest in studying the whys and wherefores of Zen. Sawaki Rōshi also used to say frequently, "Just sit—that's all there is," and "No matter how many years you sit doing zazen, you will never become anything special."

The first time I heard these two expressions I thought to myself, well, finally I can just sit without having to do anything—no more reading, no more having to answer to anyone, no more anything. Needless to say, the conclusion that I had drawn upon hearing Sawaki Rōshi's remarks was completely off the mark. Zazen is not an escape from the world. Behind Sawaki Rōshi's statements were many, many years of hard study and practice.

But of practicing what? studying what? I was only interested in sticking to the letter of Sawaki Rōshi's pronouncements, not realizing that the significance and ramifications of "just sit" went far beyond the physical act of folding one's legs and facing the wall.

Uchiyama Rōshi helped me a great deal in not allowing me to use zazen as an escape. He said, "You must know that behind zazen are the teachings of Buddhism, and behind them, your own life experience." These words went a long way in clarifying for me a passage in the *Shōbō-genzō: Genjō Kōan* (Actualizing the Koan) "To study Buddhism is to study the Self." Of course, to study the Buddha's Way includes practicing zazen. In fact, whenever the word "study" appears in Dōgen Zenji's writings, it is inclusive of or based upon practice. Dōgen says here that to study Buddhism means to study one's Self; to learn Buddhism is to learn one's Self. Until I read that passage, I thought that studying meant learning about a lot of things that I did not yet know, and actually, did not really care about. Here, however, Dōgen equates the study and practice of the Buddha's Way with the study and practice of one's Self. Looking deeply into the writings and sutras of past teachers does not mean to learn something that is unrelated to us. Studying ancient writings means to study our lives. To study the *Tenzo Kyōkun* came to mean for me that I would be studying my own life. In reading the text over and over I have found the truth in a remark made to me by the senior monk at Antai-ji at that time, "It's not reading the *Tenzo Kyōkun* that is difficult, it is doing the *Tenzo Kyōkun* that takes all you've got!"

With the advice and encouragement of that senior priest, I was able to put together the first translation of the text in about a year. The next eight years I spent refining it, which means that I have continued to practice, using the text as a guide for my own life. One who engages in translating Buddhist texts (or religious texts of any kind), first of all, should know the basis from which those texts came into existence, and secondly, to understand them well, he must become intimate with their content by practicing what they teach. Otherwise, that person merely becomes a transliterator—someone who simply exchanges the surface meaning of the letters of one language for those of another language.

At the time Dōgen Zenji was writing the *Tenzo Kyōkun*, he had already left Kennin-ji in Kyoto, and had set up his own monastery at Kōshō-ji in Fukakusa, just south of the city. At Kōshō-ji, Dōgen gained a reputation for being a strict teacher, and the number of disciples and followers increased rapidly. Hence, it was only natural that some sort of regulations be established to insure that everyone could practice with as few difficulties as possible. These regulations were born out of the situation as it developed.

Dōgen finished writing the *Tenzo Kyōkun* in the spring of 1237, at the age of 37. The remaining chapters of the *Eihei Daishingi,* which deal with other aspects of monastic life, were completed later on: *Taidaiko Gogeajari-hō* at Kippo-ji in 1244, *Chiji Shingi* at Eihei-ji in 1246, and *Bendō-hō, Fushukuhan-pō,* and *Shuryō Shingi* at Eihei-ji in 1248 or 1249. Although there are a number of versions of the *Tenzo Kyōkun,* the original text upon which this translation is based is the *Eiheigen Zenji Shingi* compiled by Reiyō Endō, and published through the Sōtō-shū Shūmuchō Kyōiku-bu in 1956.

Regarding the format of this book, I have placed the text of the *Tenzo Kyōkun* first, followed by Uchiyama Rōshi's commentary. I have added notes to the text and to each chapter where I felt them useful to anyone seeking further explanations. In the notes to the main text itself, I occasionally included passages from Uchiyama Rōshi's translation into modern Japanese in order to show the reader how a present-day Japanese teacher understands the original.

I should also add that the first chapter of Uchiyama Rōshi's commentary here is not the first chapter of Rōshi's book *Jinsei Ryōri no Hon*, from which all of the other chapters of this book were derived. The first chapter was translated from an article written by Uchiyama Rōshi for the magazine *Sanshō*, published by Daihon-zan Eihei-ji. The article was included in a special edition of *Sanshō* (November, 1978) devoted entirely to the *Tenzo Kyōkun*. It was entitled "*Tenzo Kyōkun* and *Shikan-taza*" and I felt it would function as a bridge between Rōshi's first book in English, *Approach to Zen*, which deals with the particulars of zazen, and chapters two through fourteen of this book, which deal more with our day-to-day affairs.

It goes without saying that the central practice of a person practicing Buddhism is zazen. However, the reader should not get the idea that here I am comparing zazen with the rest of our day-to-day activities. To do so would be to fall into the trap that many practitioners fall into of clinging to the *idea* that practicing zazen is most important; therefore, one should practice it twenty-four hours a day. The error here is in taking literally the idea of zazen being the most important activity in our life as opposed to all our other activities.

On the other hand, there is another trap that people can and often do fall into, and that is the one of thinking that we must practice zazen in all of our day-to-day activities. The obvious next step in this way of thinking is to equate all of one's activities with zazen. That is, everything one does is zazen—eating, sleeping, drinking, being. The practical problem in this way of thinking is that all too often people simply wind up doing less and less zazen, deluding themselves into believing that since all their activities are zazen there is no need to sit and face the wall and do zazen.

To restate the problem, taking the idea of zazen as the central practice in a relative or comparative sense leads to an egoistical extreme eventually inviting suicide. On the other hand, taking the idea of zazen in a "broader" context leads to a kind of simplistic eclecticism having nothing to do with zazen. In other words, to state that zazen has a definite and particular form, and to cling to that position leads to one kind of trouble, while stating that zazen has no particular form sends one off in another confused direction. There is no logical resolution to this problem. And it is this illogical paradox with which a true practitioner of Zen must "sit," *both* literally and spiritually.

I have tried to keep technical Buddhist expressions to a minimum to preserve the spirit of Uchiyama Rōshi's style; I have also added additional material on them when they did come up. This means, I hope, that a person knowing very little about Buddhism may pick up the book and read through it without stumbling over Sanskrit and Chinese words, I have also included a brief glossary that includes the names of the works which are mentioned in the text, and also the names of the Chinese masters who appeared either in the *Tenzo Kyōkun* or in the commentary.

In closing, I would like to thank the people who contributed to this book: Lew Warren, who was an inspiration in the early days; Shōhaku Okumura, who was kind and patient enough to go over the entire manuscript with me before the final typing, and who helped me to clarify a number of passages that had always been somewhat bewildering to me; all of the Westerners who have practiced either at Antai-ji here in Japan or at Valley Zendo in Charlemont, Massachusetts, a sister temple of Antai-ji; Jennifer Watanabe and Peter Galliott, who were kind enough to read through the manuscript at various stages of its development and to offer helpful criticism; my wife, Yūko, who never allows me to throw around Buddhist terminology but demands that I be able to express Buddhism in my own words; and Martin Nakell, to whom I would like to give special acknowledgement for his work on the manuscript.

Finally, I would like to express my gratitude to my friend and teacher, Kōshō Uchiyama Rōshi, who has always encouraged me to relook at my own Christian roots in the light of my practice of Buddhism, something that otherwise I might never have done.

THOMAS WRIGHT

Kyoto, Japan
January 1982

Instructions for the Zen Cook

Tenzo Kyōkun

From ancient times, in communities practicing the Buddha's Way,[1] there have been six offices[2] established to oversee the affairs of the community. The monks holding each office are all disciples of the Buddha and all carry out the activities of a buddha[3] through their respective offices. Among these officers is the tenzo, who carries the responsibility of preparing the community's meals.

It is written in the *Chanyuan Qinggui*[4] that "the function of the tenzo is to manage meals for the monks."

This work has always been carried out by teachers settled in the Way and by others who have aroused the bodhisattva spirit within themselves. Such a practice requires exerting all your energies.[5] If a man entrusted with this work lacks such a spirit, then he will only endure unnecessary hardships and suffering that will have no value in his pursuit of the Way.

The *Chanyuan Qinggui* also says, "Put your awakened mind[6] to work, making a constant effort to serve meals full of variety that are appropriate to the need and the occasion, and that will enable everyone to practice with their bodies and minds with the least hindrance."

Down through the ages, many great teachers and patriarchs, such as Guishan Lingyou and Dongshan Shouchu, have served as tenzo. Although the work is just that of preparing meals, it is in spirit different from the work of an ordinary cook or kitchen helper.

When I was in China, I talked in my spare time with many older monks who had years of experience working in the various offices. They taught me a little of what they had learned in their work. What they had to say must surely be the marrow of what has been handed down through the ages by previous buddhas and patriarchs[7] settled in the Way.[8]

We should thoroughly study the *Chanyuan Qinggui* concerning the overall work of the tenzo, and moreover, listen closely to what those who have done this work have to tell us regarding the details.

I shall now take up the work of the tenzo covering a period of one complete day. After the noon meal the tenzo should go to the *tsūsu* and *kansu* to get the rice, vegetables, and other ingredients for the following morning and noon meals.[9] Once he has these, he must handle them as carefully as if they were his own eyes. Renyong of Baoneng said, "Use the property and possessions of the community as carefully as if they were your own eyes." The tenzo should handle all food he receives with respect, as if it were to be used in a meal for the emperor. Cooked and uncooked food must be handled in the same manner.

Next, all the officers meet in the kitchen or pantry and decide what food is to be prepared for the following day, for example, the type of rice gruel, the vegetables, the seasoning. In the *Chanyuan Qinggui* it says: "When deciding on the amount of food and number of side dishes for the morning and noonday meals, the tenzo should consult with the other officers. They are the *tsūsu, kansu, fūsu, ino,* and *shissui.* When they have chosen the meals, the menus should be posted on the notice boards in front of the abbot's room as well as in front of the study hall."[10]

When this has been done, preparations for the next morning's meal may begin. You must not leave the washing of rice or preparation of vegetables to others, but must carry out this work with your own hands. Put your whole attention into the work, seeing just what the situation calls for.[11] Do not be absent-midned in your activities, nor so absorbed in one aspect of a matter that you fail to see its other aspects. Do not overlook one drop in the ocean of virtue [by entrusting the work to others]. Cultivate a spirit which strives to increase the source of goodness upon the mountain of goodness.[12]

Again, in the *Chanyuan Qinggui* we find, "If the tenzo offers a meal without a harmony of the six flavors and the three qualities,[13] it cannot be said that he serves the community."

When washing the rice, remove any sand you find. In doing so, do not lose even one grain of rice. When you look at the rice see the sand at the same time; when you look at the sand, see also the rice. Examine both carefully. Then, a meal containing the six flavors and the three qualities will come together naturally.

Xuefeng Yicun was once the tenzo under Dongshan Liangjie. One day while Xuefeng was washing the rice Dongshan happened to pass by and asked, "Do you wash the sand and pick out the rice, or wash the rice and pick out the sand?"[14] "I wash and throw away both the sand and the rice together," Xuefeng replied. "Then what on earth do the residents here eat?" Dongshan pressed again. In reply, Xuefeng turned over the rice bucket. On seeing that, Dongshan said, "The day will come when you will practice under another master."[15]

In this same way, the greatest teachers from earliest times who were settled in the Way have carried out their work with their own hands. How are we inexperienced practitioners of today able to remain so negligent in our practice! Those who have come before us have said, "The Way-Seeking Mind of a tenzo is actualized by rolling up your sleeves."

In order not to lose any of the rice when picking out the sand, do it carefully with your own hands. Again, in the *Chanyuan Qinggui* we find, "Pay full attention to your work in preparing the meal; attend to every aspect yourself so that it will naturally turn out well."

Next, you should not carelessly throw away the water that remains after washing the rice. In olden times a cloth bag was used to filter out the water when it was thrown away. When you have finished washing the rice, put it into the cooking pot. Take special care, lest a mouse accidentally falls into it. Under no circumstances allow anyone who happens to be drifting through the kitchen to poke his fingers around or look into the pot.

Prepare those vegetables that will be used in a side dish for the following morning's meal. At the same time, clean up the rice and leftover soup from the noon meal. Conscientiously wash out the rice container and the soup pot, along with any other utensils that were used. Put those things that naturally go on a high place onto a high place, and those that would be most stable on a low place onto a low place; things that naturally belong on a high place settle best on a high place, while those which belong on a low place find their greatest stability there.[16]

Clean the chopsticks, ladles, and all other utensils; handle them with equal care and awareness, putting everything back where it naturally belongs. Keep your mind on your work and do not throw things around carelessly.

After this work has been done it is time to prepare for the following day's noon meal. First of all, check to see whether there are any insects, peas, rice-bran, or tiny stones in the rice, and if so, carefully winnow them out.

When choosing the rice and vegetables to be used, those working under the tenzo should offer sutras to the spirit of the *kamado*.[17] Then, begin preparing the ingredients for whatever side dish and soup there might be, cleaning everything thoroughly of any dirt or insects.

When the tenzo receives the food from the *kusu*,[18] he must never complain about its quality or quantity, but always handle everything with the greatest care and attention. Nothing could be worse than to complain about too much or too little of something, or of inferior quality.

Both day and night, allow all things to come into and reside within your mind. Allow your mind (Self) and all things to function together as a whole.[19] Before midnight direct your attention to organizing the following day's work; after midnight begin preparations for the morning meal.

After the morning meal, wash the pots and cook the rice and soup for the noon meal. When soaking the rice and measuring the water, the tenzo should be present at the sink.

Keep your eyes open. Do not allow even one grain of rice to be lost. Wash the rice thoroughly, put it in the pot, light the fire, and cook it. There is an old saying that goes, "See the pot as your own head; see the water as your lifeblood."

Transfer the cooked rice into a bamboo basket in summer or a wooden container in winter, and then set it on the table. Cook the rice, soup, and any side dish all at the same time.

The tenzo must be present, paying careful attention to the rice and soup while they are cooking. This is true whether the tenzo does the work by himself or has assistants helping him either with the cooking or the tending of the fires. Even though in the larger monasteries recently people have been placed in charge of cooking the soup or the rice, the tenzo should not forget that these people are assistants working under him and cannot be held responsible for this work. In olden times the tenzo was completely in charge; there were no such assistants.[20]

When you prepare food, never view the ingredients from some commonly held perspective, nor think about them only with your emotions. Maintain an attitude that tries to build great temples from ordinary greens, that expounds the *buddhadharma* through the most trivial activity. When making a soup with ordinary greens, do not be carried away by feelings of dislike towards them nor regard them lightly; neither jump for joy simply because you have been given ingredients of superior quality to make a special dish. By the same token that you do not indulge in a meal because of its particularly good taste, there is no reason to feel an aversion towards an ordinary one. Do not be negligent and careless just because the materials seem plain, and hesitate to work more diligently with materials of superior quality. Your attitude towards things should not be contingent upon their quality. A person who is influenced by the quality of a thing, or who changes his speech or manner according to the appearance or position of the people he meets, is not a man working in the Way.

Strengthen your resolve, and devote your life spirit to surpassing the refinement of the ancient patriarchs and being even more meticulous than those who came before you. How do we apply our life aspiration so that it will function for the Way? If great teachers in the past were able to make a plain soup from greens for only a pittance, we must try to make a fine soup for the same amount. This is very difficult to do. Among other things, there are great differences between ages past and today, so even hoping to stand alongside the teachers of former times is no simple matter. Yet, being scrupulous in our actions and pouring our energy into those actions, there is no reason why we cannot equal the ancient masters.[21] We must aspire to the highest of ideals without becoming arrogant in our manner.

These things are truly just a matter of course. Yet we remain unclear about them because our minds go racing about like horses running wild in the fields, while our emotions remain unmanageable, like monkeys swinging in the trees. If only we would step back to carefully reflect on the horse and monkey, our lives would naturally become one with our work. Doing so is the means whereby we turn things even while simultaneously we are being turned by them.[22] It is vital that we clarify and harmonize our lives with our work, and not lose sight of either the absolute or the practical.

Handle even a single leaf of a green in such a way that it manifests the body of the Buddha. This in turn allows the Buddha to manifest through the leaf. This is a power which you cannot grasp with your rational mind. It operates freely, according to the situation, in a most natural way. At the same time, this power functions in our lives to clarify and settle activities and is beneficial to all living things.[23]

After all the preparations for the meal are complete, clean up thoroughly, putting everything back where it ought to be. When the drum sounds and the bell rings both morning and evening, be sure not to miss zazen nor going to see the master to receive his teaching.

When you return to your room, shut your eyes and count the number of people in the *sōdō*.[24] Do not forget the elder priests and retired monks, plus those living in single rooms. Include those in the infirmary or any other elderly people. In addition to these, any monks who are on leave and others who may have just arrived but are not yet living fully within the community should be taken into account. And finally, those living in any of the subtemples within the complex must be added. If there are any doubts, check with the heads of the offices or those in charge of the various residences where people might be staying.

When you know the exact number in the community, then calculate the amount of food to be cooked. For every grain of rice to be eaten, supply one grain. In dividing one grain, the result may be two half-grains, or possibly three or four. On the other hand, one grain might equal a half-grain or perhaps two half-grains. Then again, two half-grains might be counted as one whole grain. You must be able to see clearly how much of a surplus will be created if you add one unit of rice, or whether there will be enough if you take away one unit.

When you eat a grain of Luling rice[25] you may become the monk Guishan. When you add a grain, you may become the cow. Sometimes the cow eats Guishan, sometimes Guishan pastures the cow!

Consider whether you have thoroughly understood these matters and are able to make these calculations. Go back over everything again, and when you have understood these details be prepared to explain them to others according to their capacity to understand. Use ingenuity in your practice; see the cow and Guishan as one, not as two, even though temporarily they appear that way. In your day-to-day life, do not forget this even for a moment.

If someone comes to make a monetary donation for the food, consult the other officers concerning how that money is to be used. This has been the custom in Buddhist communities down through the ages. As for other kinds of donations to the community, such as items which will be distributed among the residents, again, consult the other officers. In other words, do not infringe on the authority of other officers or make decisions outside the boundary of your responsibility.

After each meal has been carefully prepared, place it on a table. Put on your *kesa*[26] and spread out your *zagu*.[27] Facing the *sōdō*, where everyone does zazen, offer incense and bow nine times. Afterwards, carry the meal into the *sōdō*.

All day and all night, the tenzo has to make arrangements and prepare meals without wasting a moment. If he throws all his energy into whatever the situation truly calls for, then both the activity and the method by which he carries it out will naturally work to nurture the seeds of the *buddhadharma*. Just taking care of the function of the tenzo enables all the residents in the community to carry on their practice in the most stable way.[28]

It has been several hundred years since the *buddhadharma* was introduced into Japan. Yet, no one has ever written about the preparation and serving of meals as an expression of *buddhadharma,* nor have any teachers taught concerning these matters. Much less has there been any mention of bowing nine times prior to offering the meal to the residents. Such a practice has never entered the minds of people in this country. Here people think nothing of eating like animals with no concern for the way they eat. What a pathetic state of affairs. It truly saddens me to see things this way. Why must it be so?

When I was at Mount Tiantong, a monk called Lu from Qingyuan Fu was serving as tenzo. One day after the noon meal I was walking to another building within the complex when I noticed Lu drying mushrooms in the sun in front of the *butsuden*.[29] He carried a bamboo stick but had no hat on his head. The sun's rays beat down so harshly that the tiles along the walk burned one's feet. Lu worked hard and was covered with sweat. I could not help but feel the work was too much of a strain for him. His back was a bow drawn taut, his long eyebrows were crane white.

I approached and asked his age. He replied that he was sixty-eight years old. Then I went on to ask him why he never used any assistants.

He answered, "Other people are not me."

"You are right," I said; "I can see that your work is the activity of the *buddhadharma*, but why are you working so hard in this scorching sun?"

He replied, "If I do not do it now, when else can I do it."

There was nothing else for me to say. As I walked on along that passageway, I began to sense inwardly the true significance of the role of tenzo.

I arrived in China in April 1223, but, being unable to disembark immediately, I stayed on board ship in the port of Ningbo. One day in May, while I was talking with the captain, an old monk about sixty years of age came directly to the ship to buy mushrooms from the Japanese merchants on board. I invited him for tea and asked him where he was from. He said he was the tenzo at the monastery on Mount Ayuwang and added,

"I am originally from Xishu, although I left there over forty years ago. I am sixty-one this year and have practiced in several Zen monasteries in this country. Last year, while living at Guyun, I visited the monastery on Mount Ayuwang, though I spent my time there totally confused as to what I was doing.[30] Then, after the summer practice period last year,[31] I was appointed tenzo. Tomorrow is May 5th,[32] but I have nothing special to offer the monks. I wanted to prepare a noodle soup, but as I did not have any mushrooms to put in it, I came here to buy some."

I asked, "When did you leave Ayuwang?"

He replied, "After lunch."

"Is it far from here?"

"About fourteen miles."

"When will you go back to the temple?"

"I am planning to return as soon as I've bought the mushrooms."

"You can't imagine how fortunate I feel that we were able to meet unexpectedly like this. If it's possible, I wish you would stay a while longer and allow me to offer you something more."

"I am sorry, but that is impossible just now. If I am not there tomorrow to prepare the meal, it will not be made well."

"But surely there must be others in a place as large as Ayuwang who are capable of preparing the meals. They will not be that inconvenienced if you are not there, will they?"

"I have been put in charge of this work in my old age. It is, so to speak, the practice of an old man.[33] How can I entrust all that work to others. Moreover, when I left the temple, I did not ask for permission to stay out overnight."

"But why, when you are so old, do you do the hard work of a tenzo? Why do you not spend your time practicing zazen or working on the koans[34] of former teachers? Is there something special to be gained from working particularly as a tenzo?"

He burst out laughing and remarked, "My good friend from abroad! You do not yet understand what practice is all about, nor do you know the meaning of characters."[35]

When I heard this old monk's words I was taken aback and felt greatly ashamed. So I asked him, "What are characters and what is practice?"

He replied, "If you do not deceive yourself about this problem, you will be a man of the Way."[36] At the time, I was unable to grasp the meaning of his words.

"If you do not understand, please come to Mount Ayuwang sometime and we will talk about the nature of characters more fully." With that he rose quickly. "It is getting late and the sun is about to set. I am afraid I cannot stay any longer." Then he left for Mount Ayuwang.

In July of the same year, I stayed on Mount Tiantong. One day the tenzo from Ayuwang came to see me. He said: "As the summer practice period has ended, I shall be retiring as tenzo and plan to return home. I heard that you were here and wanted very much to talk with you and see how you were doing."

I was indeed happy to see him and received him cordially. We talked about various things, and finally came to the matter he had touched on aboard the ship concerning the practice and study of characters.

He said, "A person who studies characters must know just what characters are, and one intending to practice the Way must understand what practice is."

I asked him once again, "What are characters?"

"One, two, three, four, five," he replied.

"What is practice?"

"There is nothing in the world that is hidden."[37]

Although we talked about many other things I will not mention them here. Whatever little bit I have learned about characters and practice is largely due to that tenzo. When I met again with my teacher Myōzen,[38] who later died in China, and told him of my meeting with the tenzo from Mount Ayuwang, he was extremely happy to hear about it. Later on, I came across a *gāthā* Xuedou[39] had written for one of his disciples:

> One, seven, three, five—
> The truth you search for cannot be grasped.
> As night advances, a bright moon
>   illuminates the whole ocean;
> The dragon's jewels are found in every wave.
> Looking for the moon, it is here,
>   in this wave, in the next.

It dawned on me then that what the tenzo I had met the previous year had said coincided perfectly with what Xuedou was pointing out through his *gāthā*. I realized more than ever that the tenzo was a man fully living out the *buddhadharma*.

I used to see the characters one, two, three, four, and five; now I also see six, seven, eight, nine, and ten.[40] Future students must be able to see that side from this side as well as this side from that side. Practicing with intense effort, using all your ingenuity, you will be able to grasp genuine Zen that goes beyond the surface of characters. To do otherwise will only result in being led about by variously tainted Zen that will leave you incapable of preparing meals skillfully for the community.[41]

Regarding the office of tenzo, stories such as those I mentioned previously about Guishan and Dongshan have been passed down through the ages. In addition to the monks from Mount Tiantong and Mount Ayuwang, I met and talked with monks who served as tenzo from other monasteries. If we look closely into some of these stories we will realize the meaning of characters and the nature of practice. Actually, just working as tenzo is the incomparable practice of the Buddhas. Even one who accedes to the head of the community should have these same attitudes.

In the *Chanyuan Qinggui* we find: "Prepare each meal with meticulous care, making sure there is enough. Do not be remiss in the four offerings of food, clothing, bedding, and medicine. Shakyamuni was to have lived to one hundred years of age, but died at eighty, leaving twenty years for his disciples and descendants. We today are living in the favor of this merit. If we were to receive even one ray of light emitted from the *byakugōkō*[42] between his eyebrows, we would be unable to exhaust its merit." The text goes on to say: "You should think only about how to best serve the community, having no fear of poverty. As long as your mind is not limited you will naturally receive unlimited fortune." The head of the community should generate this attitude towards serving the residents.

In preparing food for the community, it is crucial not to grumble about the quality of the ingredients, but rather to cultivate a temper which sees and respects them fully for what they are. Look at the story of the old woman who gained great merit in future lives by offering to Shakyamuni the water she had just used to wash the rice.[43] Or reflect on the final deed of King Asoka, who on his deathbed gladly offered half a date to a temple from off his table.[44] From this it was foretold that the king would reach nirvana in his next life. The true bond established between ourselves and the Buddha is born of the smallest offering made with sincerity rather than of some grandiose donation made without it. This is our practice as human beings.

A dish is not necessarily superior because you have prepared it with choice ingredients, nor is a soup inferior because you have made it with ordinary greens. When handling and selecting greens, do so wholeheartedly, with a pure mind, and without trying to evaluate their quality, in the same way in which you would prepare a splendid feast. The many rivers which flow into the ocean become the one taste of the ocean; when they flow into the pure ocean of the dharma there are no such distinctions as delicacies or plain food, there is just one taste, and it is the *buddhadharma,* the world itself as it is. In cultivating the germ of aspiration to live out the Way, as well as in practicing the dharma, delicious and ordinary tastes are the same and not two. There is an old saying, "The mouth of a monk is like an oven."[45] Remember this well.

Likewise, understand that a simple green has the power to become the practice of the Buddha, quite adequately nurturing the desire to live out the Way. Never feel aversion toward plain ingredients. As a teacher of men and of heavenly beings, make the best use of whatever greens you have.

Similarly, do not judge monks as deserving of respect or as being worthless, nor pay attention to whether a person has been practicing for only a short time or for many years. Without knowing where to find our own stability, how are we to know where someone else would be most stable? If the standard with which we evaluate others is incorrect, we are likely to see their good points as bad, and vice versa. What a mistake to make!

There may very well be differences between those who have been practicing over many years and those who have just begun, or between those gifted with great intelligence and those not so gifted. Even so, all are the treasures of the *saṃgha*. Though someone may have been mistaken in the past, he may very well be correct in the context of things now. Who is to say whether someone is a fool or a sage?

The *Chanyuan Qinggui* says: "Whether a person be stupid or wise, to the extent he is a monk, he is a treasure to all people and to all the various worlds." Even if there may be right or wrong, do not cling to that judgment. The aspiration to follow this attitude is itself the very functioning of the Way that actualizes incomparable wisdom.[46] Despite the fact that one has had the good fortune to encounter Buddhism, to follow a false step concerning this point will result in completely missing the Way.[47] The marrow of the great practitioners of former times lay in their putting this spirit into all their activities. Brothers and sisters in future generations who serve as tenzo will touch on the essence of this Buddhist teaching only when they practice in a manner consistent with this attitude. The regulations of the great teacher Baizhang Huihai[48] are not something to be taken lightly.

When I returned to Japan I stayed at the temple Kennin-ji for about two years. They had the office of tenzo, but in name only; there was no one who actually carried out the functions of the office. Since no one clearly saw that the work of the tenzo itself is the activity of a buddha, it should not be surprising that there was no one capable of functioning with conviction through this office. Despite the fact that he had had the good fortune to succeed to the office of tenzo, since he had never encountered a living example of a tenzo functioning as a buddha he was only wasting his time, carelessly breaking the standards of practice. It was a truly pathetic situation.

I closely observed the monk who was appointed to the office of tenzo. He never even helped to prepare the meals, but entrusted all the work to some absent-minded, insensitive servant, while he merely gave out orders. Never once did he check to see if the work was being done properly. It was as if he thought that watching carefully to see how the rice and vegetables were being prepared was somehow rude or shameful, like peering into the private room of a woman living next-door. He spent his time in his room lying around or gabbing with someone. Or he busied himself reading or chanting sutras. I never once saw him approach a pot, much less make any effort to obtain the necessary supplies or think at all about the overall menu of the temple. He did not know that taking care of these matters is itself Buddhist practice. Nor, apparently, did the practice of putting on his *kesa* and bowing nine times prior to serving each meal ever occur to him, not even in a dream. And, as he himself was not aware of these things, he was hardly in a position to go around teaching the younger monks, even though officially that may have been his duty. It was a pathetic and sad state of affairs.

Though a person might be fortunate enough to be appointed to the office of tenzo, if he lacks the aspiration to walk the Way, he will return empty-handed from the mountain of goodness and the ocean of virtue. Yet, though a person may not have awakened the spirit of a bodhisattva within himself, if he encounters someone who has done so it will be possible for him to practice the way of life of the Buddha. Or, even if he does not encounter an awakened teacher, if he has a deep aspiration to live this incomparable way of life, surely he will become familiar with the practice of such a Way. However, if both these conditions are lacking, how could anyone possibly function within the way of life of a buddha?

In all the many monasteries located on the various mountains I have visited in Song China, the monks holding the respective offices worked in their capacity for one year at a time, yet they always maintained and exhibited the same attitude as the head of the community, applying that attitude appropriately to the time and circumstances. The three aspects of this attitude are to see that working for the benefit of others benefits oneself; to understand that through making every effort for the prosperity of the community one revitalizes one's own character; and to know that endeavoring to succeed and to surpass the patriarchs of past generations means to learn from their lives and to value their examples.

Be very clear about this: A fool sees himself as another, but a wise man sees others as himself.[49]

As an ancient teacher has said:

> Two-thirds of our days are already over,
> And we have not practiced clarifying who we are.
> We waste our days in chasing satisfaction,
> So that even when called, we refuse to turn around.
> How regrettable.[50]

Not to encounter a true teacher will result in being led around by your feelings and emotions. The case of the foolish son of a wealthy man leaving home with the family treasure and throwing it away like so much rubbish is truly a pathetic one.[51] Likewise, to the extent that we are familiar with what the work of the tenzo is we must not squander it.

In reflecting on those who have labored as tenzo with an attitude of practicing the Way, we see that in every case the manner in which they carried out their work coincided exactly with the virtues of their character. Daigui's enlightenment came at a time when he was working as the tenzo under Baizhang.[52] The incident of Dongshan's three pounds of sesame took place when he was a tenzo.[53] Is there anything of greater value than realization of what the Way is? Is there any time more precious than the time of realizing the Way?[54]

To cite one example of a person longing for the Way, there is the boy who made an offering of sand as if it were a great treasure.[55] The case of what good fortune would befall one who made images of the Buddha and showed an attitude of reverence before them also illustrates this same spirit.[56] The duties of the office right down to the name "tenzo" are the same as they were hundreds of years ago. If the attitude and activities of the office have not changed, how can we fail by functioning as tenzo to actualize its marvelous nature and the Way in the same way those of ancient times did.

Actually, when working in any position of responsibility, not only as tenzo, but as any officer or assistant, strive to maintain a spirit of joy and magnanimity, along with the caring attitude of a parent.[57]

A joyful spirit is one of gratefulness and buoyancy. You should consider this carefully. If you had been born into some heavenly realm, you would most likely have only become attached to the pleasures of that realm, taking neither time nor opportunity to awaken the *bodhi*-spirit, nor would you be likely to feel any particular necessity for practicing the *buddhadharma*. Much less would you be able to prepare meals for the Three Treasures despite their being the highest and most worthy of all things. Neither being Śakro-devānām-indraḥ nor a *cakravartin* compares with the Three Treasures.[58]

In the Chanyuan Qinggui we find this passage: "The *saṃgha* is the most precious of all things. Those who live in this community are unfettered by the pettiness of social affairs. Such a community manifests a refined posture devoid of fabrication about the world."

How fortunate we are to have been born as human beings given the opportunity to prepare meals for the Three Treasures. Our attitude should truly be one of joy and gratefulness.

We should also reflect on what our lives might have been had we been born in one of the realms of hell, as an insatiable spirit, as some lowly animal, or as a demon.[59] How difficult our lives would be if we suffered the misfortunes of these four circumstances or any other of the eight misfortunate conditions.[60] We would be unable to practice the dharma with the strength of the community even though we had a mind to do so. Much less would we be able to prepare food with our own hands and offer it to the Three Treasures. Our bodies and minds would be bound by the limitations and afflictions of those worlds and would have to suffer their burdens.

Therefore, rejoice in your birth into the world, where you are capable of using your body freely to offer food to the Three Treasures: the Buddha, the Dharma, and the *Saṃgha*. Considering the innumerable possibilities in a timeless universe we have been given a marvelous opportunity. The merit of working as a tenzo will never decay. My sincerest desire is that you exhaust all the strength and effort of all your lives—past, present, and future—and every moment of every day into your practice through the work of the tenzo, so that you form a strong connection with the *buddhadharma*. To view all things with this attitude is called Joyful Mind.

The deeds of even a benevolent ruler disappear quickly like foam on water or the windblown flame of a candle. Rather than be as such a ruler, it would be of more value to the *buddhadharma* for you to prepare meals and offer them to the Three Treasures.

Rōshin is the mind or attitude of a parent. In the same way that a parent cares for an only child, keep the Three Treasures in your mind. A parent, irrespective of poverty or difficult circumstances, loves and raises a child with care. How deep is love like this? Only a parent can undertsand it. A parent protects the children from the cold and shades them from the hot sun with no concern for his or her own personal welfare. Only a person in whom this mind has arisen can understand it, and only one in whom this attitude has become second nature can fully realize it. This is the ultimate in being a parent. In this same manner, when you handle water, rice, or anything else, you must have the affectionate and caring concern of a parent raising a child.

Shakyamuni took twenty years off his life expectancy to care for us in later generations. What is the significance of this? It was simply a demonstration of Parental Mind. The Tathagata did not do this in expectation of some reward or fame. He did it unconditionally, without thought of profit or gain.

Magnanimous Mind[61] is like a mountain, stable and impartial. Exemplifying the ocean, it is tolerant and views everything from the broadest perspective. Having a Magnanimous Mind means being without prejudice and refusing to take sides. When carrying something that weighs an ounce, do not think of it as light, and likewise, when you have to carry fifty pounds, do not think of it as heavy. Do not get carried away by the sounds of spring, nor become heavy-hearted upon seeing the colors of fall.[62] View the changes of the seasons as a whole, and weigh the relativeness of light and heavy from a broad perspective. It is then that you should write, understand, and study the character for magnanimous.

If the tenzo of Jiashan[63] had not known the deeper implications of magnanimity, he never would have been able to help Fu Shangzuo of Daiyuan on his way toward actually practicing the dharma through his sudden burst of laughter during one of Daiyuan's lectures.[64] If Guishan had not been able to write the character for magnanimous, he would undoubtedly not have demonstrated his deep understanding before his master by picking up a piece of dead firewood and blowing on it three times before returning it to the master.[65] Nor would Dongshan, if he had not thoroughly understood magnanimity, have responded to the question of what the Buddha is by his now famous act of picking up three pounds of sesame.

Be very clear about this. All the great teachers down through the ages have learned the meaning of magnanimity not merely from writing the character for it, but through the various events and circumstances of their lives. Even now we can clearly hear their voices expounding the most fundamental truths and the ramifications of those truths for our lives. They were men whose eyes were opened to what is most vital in a life of practice, enabling us to have contact with the buddha [the Reality of life]. Their very lives manifested the sole purpose of the true Self. Whether you are the head of a temple, a senior monk or other officer, or simply an ordinary monk, do not forget the attitude behind living out your life with joy, having the deep concern of a parent, and carrying out all your activities with magnanimity.

Written by Dōgen in the spring of 1237 at Kōshō-ji for followers of the Way in succeeding generations.

How to Cook Your Life

Jinsei Ryōri no Hon

ONE

The *Tenzo Kyōkun* and *Shikan-taza*

One day Wuzhao[1] was working as the tenzo at a monastery in the Wutai Mountains.[2] When the Bodhisattva Mañjuśrī suddenly appeared above the pot where he was cooking, Wuzhao beat him. Later he said, 'Even if Shakyamuni were to appear above the pot, I would beat him, too!' "[3]

I find this story both intriguing and accessible. Here we have Wuzhao working as a tenzo in the Wutai Mountains, when suddenly one day while cooking rice, who should appear above the pot but Mañjuśrī, the bodhisattva of wisdom, the very figure enshrined in the *sōdō!* Upon seeing this, Wuzhao struck Mañjuśrī and exclaimed, "Even if Shakyamuni were to appear above the pot, I would beat him, too!"

I was ordained as a monk on the very day that war was declared in the Pacific, December 8, 1941. Throughout the entire war, I lived in harsh poverty. Afterward, things began to settle down, and other disciples of my teacher, Kōdō Sawaki Rōshi, were able to come together again, gradually restoring the semblance of a community. In 1948 and 1949 I was going through the most difficult years of my life. Despite the fact that I had been a monk for seven or eight years, I still had not figured out just what was the aim of zazen practice. It was also a time when food was scarce in Japan and many people were actually starving, a condition that most people today in the industrialized countries cannot even imagine. I thought it was great during those days to get to be a tenzo, because I could snitch a little extra food on the side. Yet, it seemed like every time my turn as tenzo came around, I would get distracted thinking about getting a little extra to eat. Inevitably, I would mess up something in my

23

work. Actually, it was not only then that something would go wrong. Whenever I would ponder over what troubled me most during those days, such as what the aim of zazen ought to be, sure enough there would be a disaster in the kitchen! During the war, I had no spare time to read through the *Eihei Shingi* nor, as an old Zen expression instructs, to carry on my practice while reflecting on myself in the light of the ancient teachings. Just after the war, about the only thing I did have plenty of was time, and when I got around to reading the passage about Wuzhao it greatly affected my attitude towards being a tenzo. When I thought carefully about Wuzhao beating Mañjuśrī when he appeared above the pot and going right on with the cooking, I felt miserable about my inability to do the same thing, even though all that appeared above my pot was some "hungry ghost."[4] I worked hard after that to chase away the ghosts whenever they showed up.

Dōgen Zenji writes that "the directly transmitted *buddhadharma* of the ancient buddhas and patriarchs is just zazen." Zazen has the highest value in our practice of Buddhism. However, in the *Tenzo Kyōkun* there are three passages which read: "The Three Treasures [Buddha, Dharma, and *Saṃgha*] are the highest and most worthy of respect of all things. . . . Given the opportunity to prepare meals for the Three Treasures, . . . our attitude should truly be one of joy and gratefulness"; and, a bit further in the chapter, "My sincerest desire is that you exhaust all the strength and effort of all your lives— past, present, and future—and of every moment of every day into your practice through the work of the tenzo."

You might conclude from studying these passages that to take up the problem of the meaning of zazen while working in the role of tenzo, or vice versa, to ponder the significance of the tenzo's work while sitting in zazen, would be the perfect way to carry on your practice. Such is not the case. When you sit in zazen, *just* sit, and when you work as a tenzo, *just* do that. It is the spirit of *just* sitting or *just* working that is common to both zazen and to the work of a tenzo. This idea of concentrating wholly on one thing is the cornerstone of the teachings of Dōgen Zenji. In Japanese, this is called *shikan*,[5] and the ramifications this teaching of *shikan* may have in our lives are important.

The purpose of this opening chapter is to examine the connection between *shikan-taza* (just doing zazen) and the work of the tenzo.

As for the latter, we have the *Tenzo Kyōkun,* which comprises the main text of this book. But, despite the fact that a great deal has been written about *shikan-taza,* there is no other writing which brings the work of the tenzo and *shikan-taza* together, and herein lies our problem. What I shall try to do is explain how I understand Dōgen Zenji's teaching of *shikan-taza,* and then take a look at the connection this has to the *Tenzo Kyōkun.*

We already know that *shikan-taza* means to just do zazen, but what does that mean, to "just do zazen"? Dōgen Zenji describes the type of zazen we do as the "King of *Samādhis.*" We can trace the word "zazen" back to the Sanskrit words *dhyāna* and *samādhi. Samādhi* is sometimes called *tōji,* to hold or see all things equally, and sometimes *tōji* (written with different Chinese characters), or in Sanskrit, *samāpatti.*[6] Another definition of *samādhi* is that mind and environment are innately one.[7] And finally, *samādhi* has been defined in this way: "The *buddhadharma* should be grasped so that mind and object become one."[8]

The problem centers around this word "mind," in Japanese, *shin.* How we understand the use of this word is naturally going to affect our understanding of zazen.

When we think of mind in its ordinary use, we usually think of the psychological mind or conscious awareness. In Sanskrit, mind used in this sense is referred to as *citta,* in which case the expression *shin ikkyōshō* would mean to gather our confused mind together and concentrate on one thing. By definition, zazen would become some sort of exercise in mental or psychic concentration, or a method for training the mind to attain a state whereby all of one's ideas or thoughts about some object would disappear, leaving the person completely unperturbed. This is the superficial implication of *munen musō,* no notion, no thought.[9] Zazen of the Theravada teachings and of the non-Buddhist teachings are of this type of psychic concentration. Any method of psychic concentration works from the assumption that our mind is always in disorder and aims to still it by doing zazen. Dōgen Zenji, however, never taught that zazen was merely a method of working to improve yourself, nor a simplistic straightening out of your own life with no concern for those around you. Dōgen once said: "Even if you have the mind of a wily fox, do not practice the Theravada way of trying only to improve yourself!"[10]

I would not want to suggest that when the word "mind" is used in

Buddhist literature it never means psychological mind or conscious awareness, but by and large it is not used in such a narrow sense. We see that this is particularly true when Dōgen Zenji used mind in a passage in the chapter entitled *Sokushin Zebutsu* (Mind is Buddha) of the *Shōbō-genzō:*

"The meaning and scope of mind that has been directly transmitted from buddha to buddha is that mind extends throughout all phenomena, and all phenomena are inseparable from mind."[11]

Mind as the directly transmitted *buddhadharma* is used in the sense of mind extending throughout all things, and of all things being included within mind. When we speak of a zazen based on the innate oneness of mind and environment, it should not be understood that zazen is a method of psychic concentration or of trying to still one's mind.

What, then, is the meaning of mind extending throughout all things, and all things being included within mind? First of all, I would like to express it in my own words and to examine how I see it applying to myself. Looking at the volumes and volumes of Buddhist teachings that had their origins in India with Shakyamuni, and which became more and more refined down through the ages, the words and expressions which arose have never been used loosely; they have almost always carried deep meaning and broad implications. For example, when this word "mind" was first used I am sure that it was used in the same psychological sense we ordinarily think of it today. However, when we come to the expression about mind extending through all phenomena and all phenomena being inseparable from mind, the implications of the word go far beyond psychology. The meaning here is total, nondualistic. It surpasses mental or psychological implications.

To talk of our being alive implies at the same time that there is also a world of phenomena in which we live. We usually assume that the world existed long before we were born and that our birth is our entrance onto the stage of an already existing world. At the same time, we often assume that our death means our departure from this world, and that after our death this world continues to exist. Within this way of thinking a fabrication is taking shape which is not the actualization of reality itself. The actuality of the world that I live in and experience is not merely a conglomeration of ideas or abstractions.

When we look at a cup that is set down between two of us, we have the feeling that we are looking at the same cup, though actually, that is not so. You look at the cup with your vision, and from a certain angle. Moreover, you see it in the rays of light and shadows that come from your side of the room. This applies equally to me as well. In a very rough sense, we proceed to separate the reality of the situation by entertaining the idea that we both see the same cup. This is what I mean by the fabrication of ideas.

In the same way, we assume that there exists a world which you and I experience in common with all other human beings, that this world existed prior to our births, and that it will continue to exist even after our deaths. But again, this is nothing more than an idea. Not only that, we wind up thinking that we live and die within this world of fabrication. This is an utterly inverted way of looking at one's life. My true Self lives in reality, and the world I experience is one I alone can experience, and not one anyone else can experience along with me. To express this as precisely as possible, as I am born, I simultaneously give birth to the world I experience; I live out my life along with that world, and at my death the world I experience also dies.

From the standpoint of reality, my own life experience (which in Buddhist terminology equals mind), and reality (which means the dharma or phenomena I encounter in life) can never be abstractly separated from each other. They must be identical. However, to take what I have just said and conclude that everything must therefore be "in my mind" (thinking, emotional, or psychological mind) would be to fall into another philosophical trap. On the other hand, to conclude that mind is totally dependent on the environment would be to relegate the matter of mind to a sort of naive realism. The teachings of Buddhism are neither a simplistic idealism nor some sort of environmentalism.

Shin, or mind, in terms of *buddhadharma* should be understood as: the mind that has been directly transmitted from buddha to buddha is that mind which extends throughout all phenomena, and all phenomena are inseparable from that mind. My personal life experience is at the same time the world of reality. Conversely, the world of reality constitutes my mind. Hence, the use of the word "mind" in this case goes far beyond having only a mental or psychological meaning. In our age, perhaps "pure life" would be a clearer expression than mind. In the daily course of things I encounter a world of phenomena, and it is through those encounters and my experience of them that I live out my life.

With the definition of mind that I have explained above, it is necessary to take another look at the expression, "The dharma should be grasped so that mind and object become one." This expression means that we must learn to see all phenomena (everything in life) from the foundation of a pure-life experience. All too often we while away our lives, creating general assumptions and ideologies out of the thoughts that arise in our minds, and, after having fabricated those ideas, we finally dissipate our life energy by living in the world we have abstracted from them. "The dharma should be grasped so that mind and object become one," means that we must see all of the worlds that our lives encompass from the foundation of our own personal life experience; our life experience is our mind. This means that all things in life function as parts of our bodies. This is also the meaning of *tōji*, holding all things equally.

Dōgen Zenji, then, did not intend that we get rid of all the delusions, fantasies, or thoughts that come into our heads during zazen. Yet, if we go about pursuing these thoughts, we are sitting in the zazen posture thinking, and not actually just doing zazen. Trying to get rid of our thoughts is just another form of fantasy. Zazen, understood as mind being innately one with all phenomena, is a means of seeing all things from the foundation of pure life, wherein we give up both pursuing thought and trying to chase it away. Then we see everything that arises as the scenery of our lives. We let arise whatever arises and allow to fall away whatever falls away.

What I have just explained is the rationale behind the passage in the *Fukan Zazen-gi,* written by Dōgen Zenji, which says:

"Drop all relationships, set aside all activities. Do not think about what is good or evil, and do not try to judge right from wrong. Do not try to control perceptions or conscious awareness, nor attempt to figure out your feelings, ideas, or viewpoints. Let go of the idea of trying to become a buddha as well."

Human beings happen to be living creatures endowed with a head inside of which thoughts and feelings appear and disappear. The occurrence of this phenomenon, even while doing zazen, is perfectly normal. In the same way that various secretions and hormones flow through the organs of the body, thoughts can be likened to secretions of the mind. It is just that if we are not careful—or sometimes even if we are!—we put these secretions into action, invest all our energy working them out, and end up crippled, unable to act or move. The most important thing to bear in mind when practicing zazen is to completely let go of everything, since secretion is nothing more than a normal function. When we do that, everything that arises can be viewed as the scenery of our lives. This has been described as "the most fundamental appearance of things."[12] *Ch'an*, in Chinese, *Zen*, in Japanese, or *dhyāna*, in Sanskrit, also carry this meaning, while later on historically, this was referred to as *jōryo*.[13] "The deep sky never obstructs the floating white clouds"[14] is yet another expression of this scenery. Finally, an expression sometimes used to describe the zazen of the Sōtō tradition, *mokushō-zen*,[15] which means to be silently illuminating, points to this scenery as well. The basis for silent illumination is to entrust everything to the posture of zazen,[16] letting go of all that comes up without trying to work out solutions for what we ought to do about this or that. This is what is called *shikan-taza*. When we do zazen with this attitude, it is no longer sitting for the purpose of fulfilling some artificial fantasy such as gaining enlightenment or improving our minds.

In the *Shōbō-genzō Zuimonki* Dōgen Zenji writes: "Sitting is the practice of the Reality of life. Sitting is nonactivity. This is the true form of the Self. Outside of this, there is nowhere to search for the *buddhadharma*."

During zazen, if we are not very careful, we are apt to doze off or daydream about something in our day-to-day lives.[17] Since both these conditions cloud over the natural purity of our life force, the essential point is to wake up from either one and return to firmly maintaining the zazen posture. This is the activity of *shikan-taza*. This practice is in itself enlightenment; it is the wholehearted practice of this enlightenment which we should carry on.

So far, I have tried to outline my understanding of *shikan-taza*. The spirit of the *Tenzo Kyōkun* coincides with what I have been talking about up to now, that is, living out the reality of pure life. The attitude of the tenzo that Dōgen Zenji writes about is one of living in the reality of pure life day by day. As I mentioned earlier, if we are not careful we are apt to smother the vitality of our lives through the fabrication of our ideas. The teachings in the *Tenzo Kyōkun* operate from the foundation of the reality of life to thoroughly cut through the ideas and homespun philosophies we so often set up and attempt to carry out, and rather, seek to truly allow that reality to function in our lives.

In the very beginning of the text, Dōgen Zenji talks about the importance of the tenzo, cutting through the notion that this work is the same as that performed by "an ordinary cook or kitchen helper," to state that "the monks holding each office are all disciples of the Buddha and all carry out the activities of a buddha." In other words, the text shows us that the tenzo practices the reality of life just as validly as those practicing zazen. In Zen, this is called practicing single-mindedly with all one's energies.[18] This attitude is completely different from the cut and dried assumptions people too often hold when looking at the world. Living by ordinary social or worldly values is a typical example of what I mean by living in a realm of fabricated thoughts and ideas, and relative values. That is why our practice consists of cutting through the ordinary social and market values of things and human beings, and of practicing with a life attitude based upon the practice of the reality of the life of one's total Self.

TWO

Concerning the Religious Life

Nowadays, the public has become familiar with the *Shōbō-genzō* of Dōgen Zenji. However, another important text also written by Dōgen, the *Eihei Shingi*, is for the most part yet unknown. Both Nishiari Zenji[1] and my own teacher, the late Kōdō Sawaki Rōshi, have said repeatedly that monks of the Sōtō tradition must treasure the *Eihei Shingi* more than the *Shōbō-genzō*. One thing I shall always remember is the time Sawaki Rōshi cautioned me to carry the *Eihei Shingi* with me whenever I traveled to different temples. He even showed me precisely how to wrap it in the pack that monks carry with them when they travel.

The reason we should value the *Eihei Shingi* so highly is because in it, Dōgen Zenji takes his disciples by the hand and teaches them about everyday religious life. In contrast to the *Shōbō-genzō*, which is a profound philosophical teaching, the *Eihei Shingi* is more of an oral teaching that guides the disciples in a more practical way.

Because of that, it may appear on the surface that it was written strictly with practicing monks in a monastic situation in mind, and that it has no bearing on the daily lives of most people. However, if we get under the surface to touch its deeper meaning, there can be no doubt that a vibrant and practical teaching has been set down; a teaching relevant to all of us, regardless of where we might be living.

The *Tenzo Kyōkun* is the first section of the *Eihei Shingi*. *Tenzo*[2] refers to the office in charge of preparing meals for the community, while *kyōkun* means teaching, so literally, *Tenzo Kyōkun* means instructions or teachings for the cook. As a book concerned with the duties of cooking, it is, in a sense, a cookbook, though it is not the type that might be used by prospective brides, for it is a profound religious work. I feel it is one of the most valuable religious texts of all time, since it deals not only with the handling of food, but also with our attitude toward all matters and people we encounter in our day-to-day lives. Even more basically, it is a text that shows us concretely how to prepare and manage our personal lives. In this commentary I have selected those passages from the text that I feel are of special importance. From them I hope we can discover together a truth beyond relativities, and can learn how to work seeing the true value of our lives.

The *Tenzo Kyōkun* is a cookbook on life, but what is the basic ingredient with which we prepare this life? For Dōgen Zenji, it was nothing other than zazen. Religious life comes into existence by our asking how we can live with zazen as the standard for our lives, while in turn being protected by zazen. Looking at it from a slightly different angle, religious life becomes vital when zazen begins to function in our everyday activities. Just how zazen functions and guides us in a down-to-earth way is what this text is about.

In this respect, the zazen of Dōgen Zenji is religious in the very deepest sense. It differs from that of any number of books on Zen flooding the market today which depict zazen simply as a method to train the *hara* (equated by some with the solar plexus, or with the *maṇipūra* chakra), or as some sort of health plan, or as a method for cultivating the mind. Rather, Dōgen Zenji's zazen is religious in the sense that it teaches us most fundamentally how to live out our own lives. Since this is a very important point, I wish to write a bit more on this subject of zazen as religion before going into the text.

In Japan, when you say zazen, people generally assume you are talking about something one does in order to gain enlightenment. That sort of idea is far removed from the zazen of Dōgen Zenji. For Dōgen, zazen could never be separated from religion. Behind zazen there had to be the Buddhist teachings, and behind them there had to be one's own life experience.

Our discussion seems to be getting a bit complex, so I will start again with an example that will be easier to understand.

I was born at the end of the Meiji era in Hongō, a district of Tokyo, which, before the great earthquake of 1923, still had traces of the Edo period.[3] At that time, there were many teachers of classical Japanese singing, and the sound of shamisens, Japanese three-stringed instruments, used to float through the streets. If the teacher were really good-looking, she would be popular with the young men who, on the pretense of studying with her, would flock to her door.

One cold winter's day two young men had a lesson with just such a teacher. After the lesson had finished, the teacher invited them to stay and talk for a while. They were delighted at this and eagerly gathered around the gaily covered *kotatsu* (foot warmer) for a chat.

Under the *kotatsu* one of the student's fingers accidentally touched the teacher's little finger, but she continued talking as though nothing had happened. Then he grasped her ring finger; still she continued unaffectedly. Next he grasped her other fingers, and finally her whole hand, which by now felt warm and was perspiring. Despite this, the teacher still appeared composed, which aroused the young man even more. He was deeply moved, thinking he had gotten one up on his friend and that he had been chosen by this beautiful woman.

Suddenly, the teacher's mother called her from the kitchen. She answered, going to see what her mother wanted. But, under the *kotatsu*, young Hachi was still holding someone's hand.

"Damn it! This is your hand, Kuma!" Hachi bellowed at his friend.

"So, it's you gripping my hand, Hachi; and I thought all along it was her. Yecch! Your hand is greasy."

"Oh yeah? Well, your nails are too long. Why don't you trim them once in a while!"

"Now what'll we do holding each other's hand?"

"Let's arm wrestle." And, so they began. . . .

Just like what happened under the *kotatsu* in this story, when talking about Zen there are many things covered over by what is called "teaching beyond letters."[4] Just like grabbing fingers one by one, you may think while doing zazen—"Wow, what a wonderful feeling! What a fantastic state of mind! Just a little bit more to go. . . . I've got it! *Kenshō!* Satori! Enlightenment!" At that very moment the good-looking beauty called the *buddhadharma* gets up and leaves. What I am trying to say here is that there is just too much stress being laid upon a satori experience disconnected from the dharma. Without the *buddhadharma*, which is nothing other than the life of the Self, as a standard, there is no way of knowing what *kenshō* or satori really is. That is what I meant earlier by saying that behind zazen there has to be Buddhism, and behind that, there must be our own daily lives.

If the family of a man who gets all caught up in zazen begins to feel that he is impossible to live with since he started sitting, even though he supposedly has had *kenshō* or satori, or if he goes around shouting at everyone as if he were something special, then I would say that it would be better for him not to sit. Or if the people around him at work look at him as if he were becoming eccentric, hinting that it would be better not to do zazen at all if he is going to get "funny," then it is clear that the person is holding onto some absurd idea under the guise of teaching beyond letters.

The most important point to bear in mind here regarding the *buddhadharma* is the expression *mantoku enman,* or perfect harmony. To have goodness emanating naturally from your character is living more truly by Buddhism than having had some so-called *kenshō* or satori experience. There should be no doubt that living out your life, acting and being in perfect harmony, is indeed living out the life of the Self.

A satori which is unrelated to your personal character is nothing more than a kind of drunkenness. It is no more than the elation you might get from taking drugs. Needless to say, this has nothing to do either with religion or with the *buddhadharma*.

Your practice of zazen must not be something separate from your own experience of your day-to-day life, nor from the overall direction of your life. Rather, in constantly working to refine and clarify your everyday life, or the life of your total Self, your practice accords with the dharma. Here zazen becomes religion. The zazen of Dōgen Zenji, along the lines I have been discussing it, is the source of the day-to-day teaching of the *Tenzo Kyōkun,* and in our daily lives, that teaching turns around to become the backdrop for zazen.

THREE

The True Form of the Self

In the previous chapter I pointed out that the zazen of Dōgen Zenji must not be something separate from our own lives nor from the *buddha-dharma*. We must not practice zazen just to have some sort of ecstatic *kenshō* or satori experience. The nature of zazen must be such that it guides our lives in the light of the most undeniable truths of life. Although the *Tenzo Kyōkun* goes into detail concerning how we are to prepare and take care of our daily lives based on this kind of zazen, we still must ask the fundamental question: What is zazen?

The following passage from the *Shōbō-genzō Zuimonki* 3:18 (Chōen-ji Edition), expresses very well what it is: "Zazen is the true form of the Self." Too often in our daily lives we lose sight of our true Selves. Zazen restores our vision. It says, in the *Genjō Kōan*, "To study the Way of the Buddhas[1] is to study the Self."

An example frequently appearing in newspaper advice columns will illuminate this. "My present marriage is an arranged one, but recently I've really fallen in love with a girl where I work. I'm in love for the first time and want to marry her. Please tell me what I should do." People often whine about some ridiculous problem like this. Perhaps I give the impression that I have not, but that is not the case. When I was young I suffered over this same kind of problem, so I am not making fun of anyone. I anguished terribly over a similar sort of thing and wound up killing two women in my life with whining.

Precisely because I had suffered through that kind of anguish, I have come to realize that the problem lies in the area of the word "really" in the phrase, "I have really fallen in love". In short, to say that you have found a person you love more than your spouse may be a fact existing as a thought or feeling in your heart, but it is not valid to equate a fact, as real as it may seem to be, with the truth. It is just self deception, and we deceive ourselves by believing that a fact existing in our minds is absolute truth.

This is just one example, but if you think about it, these and similar kinds of deceptions happen daily. Recently, young men let their hair grow long in the hippie style and parents get upset over it, telling them to cut their hair because it looks dirty. The young people, though, insist on letting their hair grow long naturally. A difference of opinion arises. Differences of opinion over hair styles are obviously not so serious, but soon larger problems begin to develop. One thing leads to another until the whole family relationship breaks down, the children leave home completely, and everyone loses all sense whatever.

Such differences of opinion occur often between young mothers and their mothers-in-law. The mother-in-law cannot stand to see the mother treat the child roughly, while the mother thinks the mother-in-law coddles the baby too much and will spoil it.

These clashes of opinions and ideas, are not limited to those between parents and children or between in-laws; they invade the international arena as well, such as in the different viewpoints of capitalism and communism. If these clashes of ideas lead to wars in the age we are living in now, they would certainly endanger the fate of all mankind. So you can see just how differing viewpoints can lead to catastrophic results.

Why is it that these differences occur? Basically, it is because we latch onto some idea as a reality and deceive ourselves into believing this reality to be the absolute truth. In meeting a particular situation, it would be fine if the same thoughts came into everyone's mind, but that is not the case. Just as one person's face is different from another's, it is only natural that the ideas which arise in everyone's minds are bound to be various. But, if we become overly attached to our ideas and proceed to take them for examples of an unchallengeable truth, the inevitable consequence will be a clash of ideas that could end in war.

Japan's first great Buddhist prince, Shōtoku Taishi, stated quite clearly in the Constitution of Seventeen Articles, "All men have minds of their own and each man's mind views things differently. When another is right, I am wrong. When I am right, others are wrong. I am not necessarily wise and others are not necessarily fools. We are all just ordinary men."

The fact that we are all just ordinary people is really the closest to the truth. That kind of understanding is surely more important than being obsessively bound to one's own ideas of justice or rightness, which will only lead to discord, fighting, and war. When we mutually get attached to and insist upon how correct we are, we get all excited and, in the international arena, end up going to war. What else can we say here other than that we have completely lost sight of the true, absolute nature of life. How better can we demonstrate our understanding of this absolute nature of things than to return to our senses. In Buddhism, sanity means to live without losing sight of the true form of the Self.

Usually we go around getting all excited over the thoughts and feelings that fill our minds. When we do zazen, we let go of all that and gain a freshness, a true sanity. That alone is the true form of the Self. When we practice zazen, we have to let go of those ideas that arise, regardless of how frightening or grandiose they might be. In doing so, our true form manifests itself naturally. In the *Tenzo Kyōkun* this is referred to as a magnanimous or big mind.

"Magnanimous Mind [or *daishin*] is like a mountain, stable and impartial. Exemplifying the ocean, it is tolerant and views everything from the broadest perspective."

In Buddhism, when the term *dai*, or big, is used, it never means big as compared to small. If we think of big in that way, it becomes only a relative comparison that reveals nothing about what big really is.

Compared with an electron, for example, a flea's balls are enormous, but comparing them to a whale, the whale is obviously much larger. Compared with the earth, a whale is very small, and compared with the galaxy, the earth is infinitesimal. If you think the Milky Way is big, it is nothing compared with the space in the universe. Is the universe then, the biggest thing? Hardly, since the scale of the universe as the largest entity is nothing more that a concept in our minds, and what are we human beings but a kind of fungus that lives on the surface of the earth.[2] So, what is big, what is small?

As long as we continue to make intellectual comparisons there is no way of telling what big is. As long as big is something set in opposition to small, it is always going to be an inconclusive thing. In Buddhism, that sort of comparative thinking is never brought up. On the contrary, big means to stop making comparisons of big and small. At the same time, it also means to stop thinking only in terms of black/white, love/hate, right/wrong, good/evil, heaven/hell, enlightenment/delusion. In other words, big means to no longer engage in or pay heed to discriminative thought.

In the passage I quoted earlier from the *Fukan Zazen-gi*[3] in which Dōgen Zenji writes, "Drop all relationships, set aside all activities," he is saying that zazen itself is Big Mind. Similarly, in the *Tenzo Kyōkun,* Dōgen says, "Having a Magnanimous Mind [Big Mind] means being unprejudiced and refusing to take sides."

The problem that arises here obviously concerns the meaning of not discriminating. In our day-to-day lives, it is impossible to live without discriminating between good and evil, likes and dislikes. To say that giving is important does not mean we go around giving our house key to a burglar, or a rifle to someone who is crazy. If a woman is willing to make love to anyone, regardless of who the man might be, she becomes nothing but a whore. We cannot act without selecting or discriminating.

Yet, how can we call people anything but senile whose thinking is so hardened that they believe their own ideas of good or evil are irrefutable, and who become so entrenched in their own way of thinking that they become buried under it. Zazen takes this senile mind, this narrow mind of ours that constantly discriminates between good and evil and throws it away. It makes the mind more flexible and capable of seeing from a broader perspective. Zazen makes the mind like a high mountain and a great ocean.

The reason I refer to the *Tenzo Kyōkun* as a "cookbook for life based on zazen" is because it shows what a religious life with an unbiased mind is in the heart of everyday affairs where it is necessary to discriminate and choose.

FOUR

Everything You Encounter Is Your Life

As I stated previously, having a Big Mind means to remain unbiased and open. It is the mind which does not stamp a fixed value on everything, nor decide on things simply by feelings or sentiments. This does not mean that we become like vegetables, knowing or understanding nothing. We have to delve more deeply than that into the significance of Big Mind.

Sawaki Rōshi used to say that you cannot exchange even a fart with another person, that you have to live your own life. This is a typical expression filled with Sawaki Rōshi's style of humor, yet how clearly it expresses the truth of life. There is no way to borrow a fart from someone else even if we are willing to add a little fart on for interest. This absolute nature of being unable to trade or exchange with another is the essence of our very own lives! Perhaps this seems quite obvious, but I question whether more than a few people recognize the absolute nature of life—even in terms of being unable to exchange so much as a fart. We have become so accustomed to the world of giving and taking that we assume it is only normal to trade with another, and we lose sight of that life wherein trading has no bearing. For example, most people now live in a society that thinks almost any problem can be solved with money. Actually, I wonder if most of us do not more or less believe that to be true. That idea, coupled with the fact that we have made "money" the actual unit of barter, has caused it to be thought of as possessing absolute value. So all our lives we busy ourselves making money and assume it is natural to struggle for wealth and status even by deceiving, cheating, and killing one another.

Here is the diverging point between the Buddhist way of life and what we generally call the way of the world: one is a world of money in which we trade and bargain with others, while the other is a world wherein trade is irrelevant and impossible, and that is the absolute world of the Self.

Our discussion has taken quite a turn from my opening comments about farts. Please take a good look at diagram 1.

Diagram 1. In life, there can
be no exchange of anything.

I apologize for not being more elegant, but to return to the example of farts, it has been said from olden times that there are basically three kinds, and they make sounds like "boo," "blat," and "shuuu." Actually, there are many more kinds, since each fart is uniquely different. In any event, this is the world in which trading or exchanging is impossible. That is, it is the world in which each of us must rely only upon ourself.

Now, let us look at diagram 2.

Diagram 2. Each person can communicate
with others through language.

Differing from the previous diagram in which the absolute nature of human life precludes any exchange with others, here we have the world of language. One aspect of our lives as human beings is that each of us has an individual head, different both in shape and content from everyone else's. In contrast to other animals, human beings have the special characteristic of being able to communicate in complex ways through language.

Further, let us consider diagram 3.

Diagram 3. We can open up a world of
communication based on thought.

Since we are able to communicate with each other through language, we can say that human beings participate in what might be termed a "world of communication." The sort of trading and exchanging back and forth, buying and selling, winning and losing that I mentioned earlier goes on in this world.

It is precisely right here that a kind of illusion or mistake arises. We communicate with one another using our heads only in a superficial way, though I am afraid we have come to yield far too much significance to this world of communication through language. We have come to assume that we are all members of this world that has developed only in our mind. This is nothing but an illusion, although this illusion has become so widespread that it is now taken as common sense.

As I mentioned in the opening chapter, the common notion of birth is that we arrive on the stage of an already existing world of human beings who communicate with one another and that one more member has been added to the repertory company. By this same sort of reasoning, dying is seen to be nothing more than leaving the stage of humanity. Thus, "life" is taken to be all the events sandwiched between birth and death. That is, this "performance" of trading and exchanging or succeeding and failing, is what most people commonly refer to as their "life."

In the world of communication, money is the standard unit of exchange, and is considered to be of highest value. All of the materialistically advanced societies today support the belief that money can solve their problems. People run frantically trying to escape from poverty, trying to get rich. Diagram 4 is an illustration of this.

Diagram 4. Since we lead our lives in a world fabricated by the mind, we flee from poverty and misfortune and chase after happiness and wealth.

This is a world in which everything is already determined. What is fortunate and misfortunate, good and evil, success and failure are prefabricated and assumed values. Since the world of language has been developed by our discriminating minds, as long as we see ourselves as just one member of this world of exchange, it is only natural that we spend our lives running towards happiness and away from pain. Despite the fact that thinking in this way is widespread, it is basically a mistake, an illusion.

The mistake is that although there is only a partial or superficial communication going on between people, we throw our lives completely into that, failing to see ourselves as anything more than members of that world. The *buddhadharma* corrects this mistaken world view and reveals a wholly different realm. Buddhist teachings focus on our absolute Self and place the greatest emphasis on the unique and fresh quality of life.

Just what is the fresh and vibrant quality of the life of this absolute Self? One thing we can be sure of is that we will never discover it in the world of trading and exchanging with others. The true Self has nothing to do with "others"; it is a Self that lives totally within itself. The world as experienced is the world which the Self alone, you alone, can experience.

When looking at the cup, you see it with your eyes, from your angle, and with your vision, while I see it with my eyes, from my angle, and with my power of vision. There is no possibility of exchanging even our separate ways of looking at a cup. None of your personal experiences can ever be the same as anyone else's. More so, then, is your way of thinking bound to be different from everyone else's.

When you are born, your world is born with you, and when you die, so dies your entire world. Your true Self includes the entire world you live in, and in this world there is no possibility of exchange.

Despite the fact that we possess a mind capable of discriminating as shown in diagrams 2 and 3, even though we are able to communicate with each other in a general sense through language, this does not mean that the true or whole Self lives only inside this world conceived in our heads. On the contrary, we must realize that our thought-producing minds are nothing more than one aspect of our total lives. Even though at a particular time or at a particular level, it appears that we are able to communicate through language, we do so only in a limited sense. Even those aspects of our experience that occur through the medium of language are, of necessity, experiences that are totally personal. The *buddhadharma* that reveals to us the absoluteness of life is like diagram 5. You and the totality of the world you live in together constitute that which I have been calling the life of the Self.

Diagram 5. We and the world we live
in together make up the Self.

Regardless of where we might find ourselves, there is only the Self, which is always the Self. Hence, the expression *yuiga dokuson*, "I alone am revered in heaven and earth."

The "world," is not some entity which exists apart from us; the "world" is where we function. Likewise, the life of the true Self is not some entity apart from our functioning and working. Everything we encounter is our life.

Our discussion has evolved a long way from the ordinary, dualistic way of seeing ourselves and our lives. However, without going through this evolution it would be impossible to comprehend any discussion on the *buddhadharma* or the *Tenzo Kyōkun*. When we change over from seeing our lives in the usual way toward viewing everything from the perspective of the *buddhadharma,* the significance of our daily activities will inevitably change as well.

Earlier I mentioned that the role of the tenzo is to prepare the meals for the community. If we see this job of cooking in the ordinary sense, that is, as being just one occupation in society, then the tenzo becomes nothing more than an ordinary cook. Or, in a broader context, if being born into the world assumes no more importance than to appear on stage as another member of society, then the meaning of life stops there. However, the function of the tenzo expressing the *buddhadharma* in terms of living out the vivid and dynamic quality of his life lives as a total Self in whatever circumstances might arise. As long as this Self is identical with its world, when we function in the role of tenzo, this functioning becomes the life of the Self. At the same time, this is the *dōjō* where we practice living the universe-ful Self.[1]

Precisely because this work of the tenzo is one of the best opportunities for practice, it is written in the *Chiji Shingi* that Guishan Lingyou, Wuzho Wenxi, Fushan Fayuan, Jiashan Shanhui, Furong Daokai and other great masters all applied themselves to it, and through their work every one of them attained the Way. If one approaches this role of tenzo with the attitude of an ordinary cook without fully comprehending this conversion of the meaning of one's daily life, it is bound to be just one hardship and frustration after another. This is undoubtedly why Dōgen Zenji wrote in the very beginning of the text:

"From ancient times, in communities practicing the Buddha's Way, there have been six offices established to oversee the affairs of the community. The monks holding each office are all disciples of the Buddha and all carry out the activities of Buddha through their respective offices. Among these offices is that of the tenzo, who carries the responsibility of preparing the community's meals.

"It is written in the *Chanyuan Qinggui* that the 'function of the tenzo is to manage meals for the monks.'

"This work has always been carried out by teachers settled in the Way and by others who have aroused the bodhisattva-spirit within themselves. Such a practice requires exerting all your energies.

If a man entrusted with this work lacks such a spirit, then he will only endure unneccesary hardships and suffering that will have no value in his pursuit of the Way.

"The *Chanyuan Qinggui* also says, 'Put your awakened mind to work, making a constant effort to serve meals full of variety that are appropriate to the need and the occasion, and that will enable everyone to practice with their bodies and minds with the least hindrance.'

"Down through the ages, many great teachers and patriarchs, such as Guishan Lingyou and Dongshan Shouchu, have served as tenzo. Although the work is only that of preparing meals, it is in spirit different from the work of an ordinary cook or kitchen helper."

I wonder if there are not many people today who suffer because they feel themselves to be poor or misfortunate, or who have an inferiority complex because they think they belong to the lowest level of society. To me, this is foolish, since they are only thinking in terms of their being but one member of society. Living out the true Self means to put away these ideas of upper or lower, success or failure, and to learn to see that everything we encounter is our life, our true Self. The expression "I alone am revered in heaven and earth," though generally referring to Shakyamuni Buddha, is not limited to him. It applies to every one of us.

When we no longer see ourselves simply as cogs in the wheel of society, and awaken to the true Self in a total sense, then the meaning of our daily lives is bound to change. There is no need to compare ourselves with those around us, nor to put ourselves into awkward and painful situations. Rather, it is vital for us to take the utmost care of that world in which we live out our total Self. This is the fundamental spirit running through the *Tenzo Kyōkun*.

FIVE

Seeing the World
Without Holding Worldly Values

There are any number of arguments these days based on the assumption that all people are seeking happiness. Perhaps this is simply because the Japanese are not familiar with looking at things rationally, but for whatever reason, whenever that rose-colored word "happiness" is brought up, there is a tendency to assume unconditionally that this is something everyone is after. If we accept the validity of everyone's desire to be happy, then we would have to inquire into what happiness is, and consider its opposite, unhappiness. But it is not my intention here to argue about what happiness is. Rather, I wish to draw attention to the following problem: the idea of seeking happiness presupposes that at present we are unhappy.

In Buddhism, this kind of dualistic thinking has no place. Previously, I talked of how it is impossible to trade even one fart, and how finally, just living out your life, regardless of the circumstances, is the absolute reality of your life. In living out the *buddhadharma*, this kind of life-attitude is essential. Usually, people think only in terms of how they can better their situation, if only a little bit, and avoid suffering. Seeing things from the perspective of the *buddhadharma* or of Big Mind means to cease engaging in this type of prejudiced, discriminative thinking and to be resolved that whatever we meet *is* our life.

When I speak of Big Mind in terms of no longer engaging in discriminative thinking I do not mean that one becomes inert. We simply cannot live day by day without discriminating. There is no human life in which there is no difference drawn between *miso* and *kuso*.[1] This is why the question arises in the *Tenzo Kyōkun* about whether one separates the sand from the rice or the rice from the sand. Apparently in olden days in China the rice polishing process was not very efficient, and there were a lot of tiny pebbles mixed in with the rice. The first thing the tenzo had to do was pick the tiny stones out of the rice before it was cooked. In this respect there can be no doubt that food fit for human consumption lies at the point where the rice has been distinguished from the stones. So, in our daily lives, we have to discriminate, but what we must not forget is the fundamental attitude grounding this discrimination: everything we encounter is our life. This is the attitude of Big Mind.

Practically speaking, just how does this work? Earlier I quoted a passage from the *Tenzo Kyōkun* regarding Big Mind: "Magnanimous Mind [Big Mind] is like a mountain, stable and impartial. Exemplifying the ocean, it is tolerant and views everything from the broadest perspective. Having a Magnanimous Mind means being without prejudice and refusing to take sides. When carrying something that weighs an ounce, do not think of it as light, and likewise, when you have to carry fifty pounds, do not think of it as heavy. Do not get carried away by the sounds of spring, nor become heavy-hearted upon seeing the colors of fall. View the changes of the seasons as a whole, and weigh the relativeness of light and heavy from a broad perspective. It is then that you should write, understand, and study the character for magnanimous."

Usually, pound and ounce are thought of as units of weight. This metaphor means, however, that you should not be swayed by the values of society nor get all excited simply because it is spring— finding yourself in favorable circumstances. Likewise, just because it is fall, there is no need to get all upset and have a nervous breakdown. Rather, see the four seasons of favorable circumstances, adversity, despair, and exhaltation all as the scenery of your life. This is what lies behind the expression "Big Mind."

I mentioned this earlier, but since it is so very important I want to stress it again. Living out your life firmly grounded in Big Mind does not mean you become dumb and mute, nor that life is devoid of the "scenery" of enlightenment and delusion, heaven and hell, success and failure, or happiness and unhappiness.

Nevertheless, living with the attitude that everything that arises in your life is the element of stability that Dōgen Zenji taught as *shikan-taza*. This is the attitude of a man practicing zazen and, at the same time, the posture (in the broadest sense of the word) of a man of Zen."

The reason we find hell or unhappiness unbearable and run around longing to escape is because we cling so strongly to the desire for happiness. Traditionally, in the East, this is seen as a demon making a plaything out of you in the same way a cat does to a mouse it has caught. Perhaps he puts us in a pot to boil or chases us up a mountain of needles. We run about all confused and the demon taunts us all the more with our own confusion.

Or to offer a more modern-day example, a man's business fails and then his wife falls ill. His child has a traffic accident, which causes a nervous breakdown. All his misfortunes seem to come at once, and in complete despair, he begins to struggle.

However, since everything—in this case, even misfortune—is our life, what is essential especially in these circumstances is to meet adversity with an attitude of equanimity. If we fall into hell, then we need the resolve to see that hell is our home. When we are being boiled in the demon's cauldron, that is where we have to do zazen. When we are pursued up a mountain of needles, we should be willing to climb that mountain hand over hand even at the risk of our life. When we throw all our life energy into whatever we might encounter, no demon can help but retreat. What a way to live!

In the *Linji Lu* (The Records of Linji) is the following passage: "The Self far transcends all things. Even if the whole universe tumbled down, I would have no misgivings. Though all the buddhas in the ten directions might appear before me, I would not rejoice. Even though the three hells might appear before me, I would have no fear, since there is nothing I dislike."

We view heaven or hell, enlightenment or delusion all with the same eye, or to put it more positively, we throw our whole lives into whatever we encounter, and that is the attitude of living out the *buddhadharma*.

When we have developed this kind of attitude toward our lives, the meaning of living day by day changes completely, along with our valuation of the events and people and circumstances that arise. Since we no longer try to escape from delusion, misfortune, or adversity, nor chase after enlightenment and peace of mind, things like money and position lose their former value. People's reputations or their skills at maneuvering in society have no bearing on the way we see them as human beings, nor does a certificate of enlightenment make any impression on anyone. What is primary and essential is that as we develop this vision, the meaning of encountering the things, situations, or people in our lives completely changes.

The *Tenzo Kyōkun* shows us in a concrete way just how to cultivate this attitude through careful handling of the food we use to prepare meals. We must no longer look at things in the way they are commonly seen. Rather, we need to face everything that arises with the entire meaning and value of these encounters completely altered, seeing everything as our life! It says: "When you prepare food, never view the ingredients from some commonly held perspective, nor think about them only with your emotions."

In other words, you should not consider something precious simply because it cost a lot of money, nor treat it roughly because it was inexpensive. It goes on: "When making a soup with ordinary greens, do not be carried away by feelings of dislike towards them nor regard them lightly; neither jump for joy simply because you have been given ingredients of superior quality to make a special dish. By the same token that you do not indulge in a meal because of its particularly good taste, there is no reason to feel an aversion towards an ordinary one."

The tendency of ordinary cooks is to handle plain food carelessly and rich food carefully. As one practicing the *buddhadharma* in the role of the tenzo, you should prepare food with all the ardor of your life and with wholehearted sincerity.

When you think about it, to all of us practicing the dharma, the *Tenzo Kyōkun* is a remarkably compassionate text. This teaching shows us how to discover a deeply refined religious life through our daily activities.[2] The text continues: "Your attitude towards things should not be contingent upon their quality. A person who is influenced by the quality of a thing, or who changes his speech or manner according to the appearance or position of the people he meets, is not a man working in the Way."

Since the *Tenzo Kyōkun* shows us how to handle the ingredients we are about to use to prepare a meal, it follows naturally that the first thing it emphasizes is to be conscientious towards the ingredients and to prepare food with our whole hearts and minds. If our discussion stops here, however, this teaching is apt to be little different from instructions given by any head chef. To move one step further, we encounter the depth of the *buddhadharma* when we no longer become swayed by the way people ordinarily value things and do not lose sight of the absolute uniqueness of our lives. This attitude is not limited to objects; it extends to all people and situations that arise in our lives. I am sure you can understand now why I refer to the *Tenzo Kyōkun* as the "cookbook for life."

There seems to be a very strong tendency in human beings, either conscious or unconscious, to humble themselves before people they think might be beneficial to them, and to speak condescendingly to those they consider to be below themselves.

Despite the fact that most people depend on some organization only for their livelihood, the executives and higher-ups of these organizations behave arrogantly towards those under them. They are truly a comical sight, yet this situation is the norm. The *Tenzo Kyōkun* shows us that such an attitude is far distant from that of a person who intends to live out the *buddhadharma*. It illuminates for us just what the attitude of our day-to-day religious life ought to be.

Since the following passages express this same idea, I would like you to appreciate fully just how vital it is not to be turned around by ordinary social values: "When the tenzo receives the food from the *kusu,* he must never complain about its quality or quantity, but always handle everything with the greatest care and attention. Nothing could be worse than to complain about too much or too little of something, or of inferior quality. . . . A dish is not necessarily superior because you have prepared it with choice ingredients, nor is a soup inferior because you have made it with ordinary greens. When handling and selecting greens, do so wholeheartedly, with a pure mind, and without trying to evaluate their quality, in the same way in which you would prepare a splendid feast. The many rivers which flow into the ocean become the one taste of the ocean; when they flow into the pure ocean of the dharma there are no such distinctions as delicacies or plain food, there is just the one taste, and it is the *buddhadharma,* the world itself as it is."

In other words, when we live out our lives to the fullest, there is no such thing as superior or inferior, good circumstance or bad, fortune or misfortune. There is only the one taste of the great ocean of life. "Similarly, do not judge monks as deserving of respect or as being worthless, nor pay attention to whether a person has been practicing for only a short time or for many years."

SIX

On Parental Mind

In the previous discussion I talked about Big Mind, whereby everything we encounter inevitably becomes our life, as soon as we throw out our ordinary way of viewing things. Usually, we set up a world in opposition to our self, and then go about trying to pocket for ourselves as much wealth, power, or happiness from that world as we can. When our way of life accords with the *buddhadharma,* we no longer construct a world in opposition to what we think of as our "self." Rather, we see that the whole world is the true Self. This path is the way of the dharma. Since there is no longer an "other" to be dependent upon, we have neither a need to be swayed by someone or something we think exists outside ourselves nor do we long for things that we project as being apart from ourselves.

In the *Suttānipata* there is a passage which says: "Not to rely on others is to be unmoved. (752)" Here is where we find true peace of mind. When Shakyamuni became fully enlightened he is reputed to have said, "I attained the Way simultaneously with the whole world and all sentient beings. Everything—mountains, rivers, trees, grasses—all attained Buddhahood."

The following similar passage is from the *Lotus Sutra:* "The 'three worlds' are mine and all sentient beings in them are my children."[1] In other words, Big Mind as awareness that the whole world is one's true Self is the foundation of the *buddhadharma.*

Sawaki Rōshi used to use the expression, "Live the Self that fills the whole Universe." When we see the words universe, or world, or all sentient beings, we are apt to think that this means we should meditate on our awareness expanding in some large space in the way a balloon expands when filled with air. But that is not what the rōshi meant. Life must take the form of living activity, and the *Tenzo Kyōkun* teaches us that the Self inclusive of the whole world is nothing other than the very things, people, or situations that we presently encounter and know, and helps us to discover our lives through these things, and, in turn, pour all our life ardor back into them: "Once he has these [ingredients], he must handle them as carefully as if they were his own eyes"; and "Both day and night, allow all things to come into and reside within your mind. Allow your mind (Self) and all things to function together as a whole."

Big Mind, then, is not a matter of meditating on some vast, floating, spatial dimension. Rather, it is the practice of entirely devoting your life to each and every thing that you encounter, no matter what it might be.

This past summer a certain university professor came to stay here at Antai-ji. Now, as long as one stays here, whether he is a college professor or the president of some large company, he is just a practitioner like everyone else. This fellow refused to work alongside everyone else and when everyone was working in the garden or chopping wood he would be off reading a book somewhere. He claimed he was not any good at doing physical labor and said reading would be his work.

I explained to him in no uncertain terms that we do not call reading work. We grow an eggplant or make a piece of firewood with the physical labor of our bodies. Reading does not help plants grow, nor does it get the wood chopped up. Reading is reading and work is work.

He finally wound up choosing the easiest task he could find— sweeping the leaves along the temple path and gathering them into a big pile to burn. I happened to pass by the place he chose to burn them, and sure enough, he had picked out a spot directly under the camellia hedge. The flowers were being scorched brown by the heat and smoke. I had him put the fire out immediately; but here was a fellow who, while the fire was burning right under his nose, could not even see where the heat and smoke were going. How can you assign work to a person like this?! I can just imagine all the intellectual professors like him who are unable to cope with the challenge and sharper wits of today's college students.

Zen is often thought to be a state of mind in which you become one with your surroundings. There is an expression which says that mind and environment are one.[2] Enlightenment is understood as falling entranced into some rapturous state of mind in which external phenomena become one with one's Self. However, if such a state of mind were the spirit of Zen, then one would have to still one's body in order to achieve it, and never move. In order to do that, a person would have to have a considerable amount of spare time with no worries about where the next meal was coming from. What this would mean, in effect, is that Zen would have no connection with people who have to devote most of their time and energies just to making a living.

Zazen as true religion can hardly be considered the hobby of rich and leisurely people. The wonderful point of Dōgen Zenji's practice of zazen is that it is religion which must function concretely in one's daily life. He taught through the office of the tenzo, which he felt to be indispensible in a Buddhist community and which requires physical work, because he felt that zazen as religion must never be relegated only to those seeking to indulge in some rapturous state of mind.

The expression "mind and enviroment are one" is accurate, but it does not mean getting lost in a state of drunken ecstasy. Rather, it means to put all your energy into your work. That is also the meaning of *shikan*.[3]

"There is an old saying which goes, 'See the pot as your own head; see the water as your lifeblood.' " Another passage, a few paragraphs previous to the one above, says: "Clean the chopsticks, ladles, and all other utensils; handle them with equal care and awareness, putting everything back where it naturally belongs."

To "handle them with *equal* care and awareness" is very important. In other words, when you work with some tool or utensil you should put it back when you are finished with it and not just leave it sitting around. When you put a pot down roughly, banging it around on concrete or a tiled sink, it cries out in pain. If you still are unable to hear that cry, then you can hardly be said to be a person living out zazen in your daily life.

Of course, this applies not only to utensils and things, it applies equally to situations and people. A person can hardly be said to have a religious attitude who treats a teacup carefully, almost piously, simply because it is expensive, yet who feels nothing in treating people roughly. We should always strive to treat objects, affairs, and particularly people, with good care. When we begin to see that our every encounter constitutes our lives, or to put it another way, as we begin to understand the deeper ramifications of Big Mind in our lives, this mind or attitude naturally begins to function as the mind of a parent in regard to everything we meet.

"*Rōshin* is the mind or attitude of a parent. In the same way that a parent cares for an only child, keep the Three Treasures in your mind. A parent, irrespective of poverty or difficult circumstances, loves and raises a child with care. How deep is love like this? Only a parent can understand it. A parent protects the children from the cold and shades them from the hot sun with no concern for his or her own personal welfare. Only a person in whom this mind has arisen can understand it, and only one in whom this attitude has become second nature can fully realize it. This is the ultimate in being a parent. In this same manner, when you handle water, rice, or anything else, you must have the affectionate and caring concern of a parent raising a child."

A good part of the reason people treat things roughly and are hard on others is because they are thinking only of what is beneficial to themselves, or else because they dislike putting all their energies into their work.

The prefabricated houses going up everywhere in Japan today look fine for a couple of years, but then they begin to look like chicken coops. The realtors who build them are thinking only of their own profit. They have no trace of feeling for viewing their work as a parent sees its child.

Then too, there is that grandiose expression of Japanese bureaucrats, "The State is our boss." Those civil servants who work in the government receive their monthly salaries without fail, they get their bonuses, and, if they serve for a long enough time, they receive retirement grants plus monthly pensions! Since they have no feeling of urgency concerning where their next meal is coming from, they grow completely sodden with little desire to serve the people who come to them with their problems. They do their work sticking to the book and collect their paychecks. Perhaps I am prejudiced because I have never worked at a job with a fixed income. During my adult life, I have lived from day to day going out on *takuhatsu* (mendicant begging)[4] with a constant sense of urgency. So, when I come across bureaucrats and the kind of bureaucratic attitude that prevails in this country, I get very annoyed.

If these public officials truly felt their lives were worth something, they would naturally see their work as their "child," forget about their personal inconvenience, and endeavor to help those who come to them. I have felt this way for some time, and if you, the reader, just happen to be a public official not like those I have been describing, then that, of course, is quite fine. In fact, everyone hopes there might be more officials who are conscientious about their work. Devoting the whole of life's ardor to all the circumstances and people we encounter in our lives in the same way we devote ourselves to our own children is precisely how we shall find the true meaning of life.

Even in loving a child, I do not mean that we should continually pander to its every whim. Living with a Parental Mind also means to be prudent and aware of the child's real needs, lest we stifle the child with blind love. The *Tenzo Kyōkun* teaches us in detail about the active functioning of this kind of mind or attitude.

SEVEN

Having a Passion for Life

Sawaki Rōshi often said: "In the Theravada school of Buddhism any act is pardonable providing the motive is good. However, in Mahayana Buddhism, if the result is bad, there is no pardon for the act despite one's good intentions. Since the overall practice in Mahayana Buddhism must be good, there's no room for carelessness."[1] The difference between Theravada and Mahayana, then, is that in Mahayana Buddhism, life[2] is the most essential matter.

For example, for amateur farmers like ourselves, it is only natural to want the vegetables in the field to grow as rapidly as possible. We assume that the best thing for them is to receive a lot of fertilizer as often as possible. But since these plants are living organisms, they are capable of absorbing only so much; so, in our impatience, we wind up burning the roots. Here, despite our good intentions of wanting to see the plants grow quickly, the result is disastrous; we have killed the plants! Now, in Theravada Buddhism, since the motive was good, the deed would have been viewed as good even though the plants died. However, in Mahayana Buddhism, since our focus is on life, even if we lack knowledge about it, and foolishly go about killing the plants, the deed is considered to be the same as if we had no intention of growing the plants in the first place.

This is an area where we have to appreciate the spirit of the Mahayana teachings and understand the deeper meaning and significance of performing living activity. Killing crops with overfertilization is one thing, but I wonder if a similar sort of situation does not exist in regard to child education today. Recently, the expression "education-crazy mama" has come into vogue here in Japan, so I do not think that I am that excessively concerned with the matter. There are just too many things we are able to take care of nowadays simply by pushing a button or flipping a switch. We go from day to day handling machines and working with things that are in themselves lifeless, hardly ever taking a close look at what is really alive.

In dietetics, a menu is drawn up based on the calculation of the number of calories each food contains, and then estimating the total number sufficient for one day. There must be thousands of people who cannot see the forest through the trees and who faithfully follow the letter of these diet books thinking they are right in line with the newest knowledge in the field of dietetics. But from the standpoint of life in the Buddhist sense, could there be anything more hazardous than this? The human stomach is a living organism and not the same as some laboratory test tube. It might very well be possible to obtain the measurements you are after by combining so many grams of various chemicals and mixing them together in a test tube. But there is no reason to expect that the stomach will respond according to such simple arithmetic equations as $1 + 1 = 2$. First of all, human beings have an appetite as well as a capacity to digest and absorb food which varies with every person's physical constitution. It is ridiculous to pay so much attention to the way many of these so-called dietitians these days write concerning a specific amount of food being sufficient because of some calculation which demonstrates that it contains so many calories. No matter how much is said about a minimum standard requirement sufficient for a "normal" child or adult, it is unreasonable to try to force someone to eat that much if they have no appetite. By forcing people to eat you are very likely to help them ruin their entire digestive tract. Or, looking at it from a different angle, if we take people whose systems simply are not able to absorb all the nutrients from the food they eat, even if it is said that the diet provides the necessary number of calories and sufficient amount of nutrients, they are not, in fact, getting enough. So, it is not illogical to expect results like $5 + 7 = 10$, or perhaps $2 + 3 = -10$!

Present-day scientific knowledge all too often does not look at the life of each individual person, but rather tends to lump all people together. $A = A$ and a human being is a human being. Trying to apply some uniform scientific average to every individual is just too crude a way to treat people. Frankly, I wonder if science might not in fact be one of the great superstitions of the twentieth century, as well as its greatest tragedy.

Recently in Japan, bookstores are crammed with encyclopedias, literary anthologies, and educational picture books for children. When I was a child my father bought a complete collection of children's literature comprising forty or fifty volumes for my brother and myself. However, we only read one or two, while the rest ended up being burnt in the Great Kantō Earthquake disaster in 1923. At that time, we simply were not ready to absorb and digest so much. Moreover, our father engaged a private teacher for us from elementary to junior high school. In those days, this was quite unusual. When I look back on it now, I certainly do not think it was a good idea, since it only nurtured a feeling of dependence. And the reason for this was because we were forced to study before our desire to do so had really awakened.

When I see all these literature anthologies for children along with the employment of private tutors, which has become so popular now, I am concerned as to whether they are only for the satisfaction of these "education-crazy mamas," who are not taking into account the ability of their children to absorb and digest so much material, especially since most of this material only crushes the child's desire to study and fosters a sense of dependence on others. Machines may very well function in accordance with your calculations, but you should be aware that life in its broadest dimensions is surely capable of yielding a result quite contrary to the one you calculated.

In *Tenzo Kyōkun* we find the following passages: "Do not be absent-minded in your activities, nor so absorbed in one aspect of a matter that you fail to see its other aspects. . . . Future students must be able to see that side from this side as well as this side from that side. Practicing with intense effort, using all your ingenuity, you will be able to grasp genuine Zen that goes beyond the surface of characters. To do otherwise will only result in your being led about by variously tainted Zen that will leave you incapable of preparing meals skillfully for the community."

So abundant are the current examples of one-sided devotion which have resulted in losing sight of the wholeness of life. First, there is modern science as a cure-all for all our problems. Then comes the fanaticism of the so-called "new religions" (basically, a post-World

War II phenomenon in Japan) and, finally, there is the violence generated by the radical student movements in the late 1960s and early 1970s in Japan.

I feel that one factor contributing to this problem is that particularly the younger generation of today has been largely brought up with the check-the-right-answer type of education, with little emphasis placed on development of one's own creative, intuitive, and thinking powers. For example, "Which of the following do you believe in? Choose one. Soka Gakkai, Watch Tower, Yoyogi/Anti-Yoyogi [two radical student groups active in Japan in the late 1960s]." Things are laid out in black and white. There is little inspiration to sit down and probe and discuss matters, along with very little desire to raise the level of one's own knowledge. Unfortunately, this forcing of one's fanaticism on others only seems to be growing. The minds of young people who become like this have already become senile in the sense that they are hardened to others' ideas.

It is fundamental that you put your energy into the wholeness of life, before you get carried away by a single aspect or a single view of a situation.

In a book by Godō Nakanishi there is a story about how a bird hatches its eggs. While the female bird warms the eggs, she periodically gets up, turns them over with her beak, and sits down again. The eggs will not hatch well if she only warms one side and leaves the other side cool. Yet, it does not appear that she turns the eggs over because she thinks consciously that it is time to do so. Rather, she seems to do it because as she sits on the eggs her abdomen gets very warm and by turning the eggs over she can cool herself by pressing her abdomen on the other, relatively cool side of the egg.

Our passion for life works in this same way. When your passion embraces the wholeness of life you naturally look around to see what is cool and needs to be taken care of. This feeling of passion that arises naturally is the activity or the function of our lives.

What often prevents us from seeing and taking care of our life in its widest dimensions and covers over our passion for life is fanaticism—political, philosophical, as well as the following of a blind devotion to some new discovery or knowledge about one aspect of a subject. It is not that new discoveries or knowledge are in themselves bad; but blind faith and devotion to any particular thing eventually leads to the stifling of life as a whole. You have to see everything that you learn from the foundation of the life of the Self: "Future practitioners must be able to see that side from this side as well as this side from that side." When your actions arise out of the wholeness of life, then you will be able to comprehend that passion which functions in all things and constantly moves in the direction of life. Only here will you be able to find the greatest stability for your life. This is also referred to as *ichimi zen*, or genuine Zen. If you fail to see life as a whole, you will become trapped by narrowing views or philosophies, or by some blind fanaticism. In the *Tenzō Kyōkun* this is called "being led about by variously tainted Zen," which leaves you incapable of using a skillful hand to prepare or manage the life of the Self.

The quality or nature of the zazen which Dōgen Zenji teaches is a stability wherein life simply *becomes* life. At the same time, in the *Tenzo Kyōkun* he teaches us about a functioning through which life *actualizes* life.

EIGHT

Direction and Goal

About 1,400 years have passed since Buddhism came to Japan, and today the country is thought of as a Buddhist one. Yet I have heard that when non-Japanese ask what sort of religion Buddhism is, they think it rather strange when no one can give them a clear answer. And it is not only that, for few Japanese themselves have true faith in Buddhism, usually knowing at best no more than the name of the temple at which their ancestors are buried. What is the reason for this? Perhaps the major one, which cannot be easily explained away, is the laziness and negligence of the priesthood.

Yet I think a further reason which cannot be ignored is that the religion is very profound and difficult to understand. It is easy to comprehend the idea of there being such and such a god, with a certain teaching, who, if you follow that teaching, will bestow divine favor on you and guarantee your ascent into heaven. And, on the contrary, if you do not follow the teaching you will suffer, be unhappy, and wind up in hell. Such a teaching, which fixes misfortune and hell as bad and happiness and heaven as good, coincides exactly with man's egocentric desires. It is only natural that this "faith" is going to appear quite clear. However, as I stated earlier, faith in Buddhism is the ability to recognize happiness and unhappiness, heaven and hell, all with the same eye, and to live out the life of one's total Self despite the circumstances that arise. This is an area which does not quite fit into the expectations of man's egocentric desires.

What I am about to discuss next is contradictory and something which would undoubtedly have been difficult for Japanese in feudal times to understand, since the prevailing trend in those days was to keep the people ignorant, forcing them to be dependent on the government. Nowadays, however, the level of education in Japan regardless of a person's social status has risen markedly. In addition, the times now are also very prosperous. I have no doubt that readers today will be able to read Buddhist teachings with a more sympathetic eye, and that people will not only realize the profound subtleties of Buddhism, but also be able to awaken to its functioning in their everyday life.

In the *Shushō-gi*[1] are the following two passages: "Since everything is impermanent, there is nothing that can be relied upon. Like a dew-drop on a blade of grass along the path that vanishes quickly, who knows when this life will end. This body is surely not my possession. Life, changing in time, does not stop even for an instant." This second passage follows somewhat later: "Ultimately, the law of cause and effect operates clearly and impartially apart from my will. Without exception one who commits evil actions falls, while one who performs good, prospers."

If we look closely at these two statements they are completely contradictory. The first statement is about impermanence. Everything is continually changing, which means that nothing, neither wealth, health, nor children, can be accumulated. If you have these accumulations as a goal you will eventually be disappointed. The second statement introduces the world of cause and effect: a good cause will yield a good result, and a bad cause will yield a bad one. The result of one action influences the next. Now how are we to interpret these two completely contradictory statements?

Here is caricature of a life style perhaps not so dissimilar to that of any number of people in the world today: A young man awakens to his own life and starts thinking about what he should do with it. He figures everything is impermanent, life is short, and who knows when he is going to die. He concludes that the best way to live is do whatever one likes and when one reaches the end of the road, just die. So he goes ahead doing what he wants, indulging in anything and everything. Finally he runs out of money and contracts tuberculosis and venereal disease. He figures his time is just about up so he decides on one last fling—a bank robbery. While committing the robbery he attacks someone with a knife and soon after gets arrested. After his arrest, he tries to commit suicide by biting off his tongue, but fails in his attempt. He is given seven years and serves his time all the while suffering from T.B. and venereal disease. After his release, society turns its back on him because he is an ex-convict, and he himself has lost both the courage to continue his wretched life and that to commit suicide.

Here is a person who constructed his view of life mistakenly thinking only in terms of impermanence. Concluding that life is short and no one knows when they are going to die, he became desperate, and just then the law of cause and effect came to the forefront. Sleeping with prostitutes and living a life of dissipation resulted in his contracting V.D. and tuberculosis; his becoming a robber resulted in his being an ex-convict; and when he could no longer take his own life he had to suffer the consequences of all his previous actions.

However, a man who sees only in terms of cause and effect, who thinks that what life is all about is the acquisition of money and health, and devotes his life to that purpose alone may die in an instant in a traffic accident. No matter how strong he has become through exercise and body building, it is going to be of no use against a dump truck.

All of us must know one or two examples like the following: Parents place all their hope in a child who turns out to be a thankless bum, throwing away the family fortune, forever causing his parents grief. Finally, they regret ever having brought that child into the world.

When you place too much emphasis on cause and effect, impermanence is very likely to pop up, or else cause and effect work out in some weird, unexpected way. When we run into examples of this kind of life style, we certainly can become confused as to just how we should live out our lives.

In Buddhism, the view which only sees living in the world as impermanent and our trying to accumulate anything as useless is referred to as *danken;* whereas a way of life which assumes that things must be accumulated and is based solely on setting up the limited goals of wealth, good health, or offspring, is called *jōken.*[2] Both of these views, *danken* and *jōken,* are understood to be one-sided. This understanding brought about the exposition of the Middle Way.

Middle Way does not mean halfway. Nor does it mean some sort of watered-down, defeated compromise or shallow eclecticism. Rather, Middle Way means to accept this contradiction of impermanence and cause and effect within your own life. To accept this contradiction means to forbear and overcome it without trying to resolve it. At its very essence life is contradiction, and the flexibility to forbear and assimilate contradiction without being beaten down by it nor attempting to resolve it *is* our life force.

To express this concretely in terms of our daily attitude, it means to live without projecting goals while yet having a direction. Since everything is impermanent, there is no way of telling what might happen to us in the next instant—we could very well die! To set up a goal or purpose is to invite disappointment by seeing things move in a direction contrary to these goals. Yet, we are certainly in trouble if we decide that since we have no future goals or expectations there is no present direction. The *Tenzo Kyōkun* teaches that we must prepare for the next morning the night before: "Next, all the officers meet in the kitchen or pantry and decide what food is to be prepared for the following day, for example, the type of rice gruel, the vegetables, the seasoning. In the *Chanyuan Qinggui* it says, 'When deciding on the amount of food and number of side dishes for the morning and noonday meals, the tenzo should consult with the other officers. . . . When they have chosen the meals the menus should be posted on the notice boards in front of the abbot's room as well as in front of the study hall. When this has been done, preparations for the next morning's meal may begin.'"

In this seemingly matter-of-course passage there is an extremely vital teaching to be found. In this world of impermanence, we have no idea of what may occur during the night; maybe there will be an earthquake or a disastrous fire, war may break out, or perhaps a revolution might erupt, or we ourselves could very well meet death. Nevertheless, we are told to prepare the gruel for the following morning and make a plan for lunch. Moreover, we are to do this as *tonight's work*. In preparing the meal for the following day as tonight's work, there is no goal for tomorrow being established. Yet, our direction for right now is clear: prepare tomorrow's gruel. Here is where our awakening to the impermanence of all things becomes manifest, while at the same time our activity manifests our recognition of the law of cause and effect. In this routine matter of preparing tomorrow's gruel as this evening's work lies the key to the attitude necessary for coping with this absolute contradiction of impermanence and cause and effect.

Much too often we go about our lives holding on to some future goal without thinking about our present direction, or about the direction of our lives as a whole. When we stop projecting goals and hopes in the future, and refuse to be led around by them, yet work to clarify our lives, that is, the *direction* of the present, then we will discover an alive and dynamic practice. At the juncture of this contradiction we will begin to understand the function of the tenzo.

NINE

Making Life Calculations

I have been discussing the teachings of Dōgen Zenji whereby in this world of impermanence and cause and effect we are to prepare the gruel for tomorrow as this evening's work. Although we no longer go about anticipating some future happiness or goal, we live out our lives with our present direction clearly defined. This is a truly essential life-attitude.

While usually we spend most of our time chasing after money, a good reputation, or happiness, and place the meaning of our lives in the pursuit of these things, ironically, it is within this very pursuit that we suffer. What we are actually doing is setting up and comparing our present lives with goals such as money, fame, and happiness. Wanting money is premised on the assumption that we think ourselves to be poor now. We desire to become famous or be recognized because we feel we were born of low status. And we seek happiness because we have fixed on the idea that we are not happy now. While pursuing these goals we place our present life in contrast to them. In effect, our lives become dependent on these goals, so that there is no way for us to truly give expression to our lives.

In this context, giving expression to life means that a violet blooms as a violet and a rose as a rose. However, we are apt to start thinking that despite the fact that we happen to be a violet we want to bloom like a rose because we think roses are beautiful. By pursuing this sort of foolishness, we go about presuming to be unhappy. Men put up a front by pretending to be something they are not, while women spend hours preening themselves trying to look like roses when they are violets, or vice versa. Since we are only who we are, we become lonely by trying to make ourselves into something we are not. Some people who see through their own pretentiousness develop an inferiority complex or neurosis and wind up in a mental institution without ever opening the flower of their own nature.

Why is it that prior to World War II sanitoriums for patients with tuberculosis were overcrowded, while today mental institutions are flourishing? I think one reason for this, at least in Japan, is because so many people who had been accustomed to a bucolic life rushed into the cities where the life style was so gay and luxurious. Many of these people became mesmerized by the neon lights and confused by all the activity, and frittered away their lives in pursuit of some strange delusions with which to satisfy their own vanity. I cannot help feeling that the teaching of Buddhism as an attitude or posture of living the life of the Self without trying to juggle one's present life around the pursuit of some future goal is especially significant for today's generation. In this present "age of the masses," if we become absent-minded for even a little bit, we are very likely to get torn apart by the difficulty of having to make choices.

On hearing that it is only natural for a violet to bloom as a violet and a rose as a rose, some people immediately begin to wonder about whether they are a rose or a violet. Since life is always potential, whether you are a violet or a rose simply is not something that is fixed, nor is it necessary to try to figure it out. What is vital here is that you give expression to the flower of your Self, the flower of here and now, and allow it to blossom as completely and as naturally as it can in every moment of your life. That flower of your Self, that flower of here and now, is your life!

Again, you have to be careful not to misinterpret Self to mean a kind of self-centeredness or false individualism. As I have mentioned earlier, in Buddhism, your true Self includes the world you live in. In this same way, living now does not mean a directionless living for the moment. In Buddhism, the present includes both past and future.

To express it in simpler terms, I am speaking of a present which contains direction, wherein you prepare tomorrow's gruel tonight. It is not a present which relies on tomorrow's happiness. Rather, it is like the line in an old Japanese poem:

> I don't know if the autumn will bring rain or storm,
> still, I shall pull the weeds in the rice paddy.[1]

To describe this, I sometimes use the expression "just be here," in the sense of "having an overall view." That is, it is the *here* that underlies the passages: "Do not be absent-minded in your activities, nor so absorbed in one aspect of a matter that you fail to see its other aspects," and "Future practitioners must be able to see that side from this side as well as this side from that side."

To live out the life of the Self, always in the present and always where you are, is neither to shut yourself up inside some small egoistical shell trying to escape from the world, nor to become enraptured in some stilted world of Zen.

We have to exhaust all our effort to manifest and actualize eternity at this point where our Self encounters all matters here and now, and to devote ourselves to move in that direction whereby the whole world becomes settled within itself. As is written in the *Shōbō-genzō: Yuibutsu Yobutsu* (Only Buddha Recognizes Buddha): "All the buddhas of all generations have completed their practice and attained the Way. They have already attained enlightenment. How, then, are we to understand the unity of ourselves and the buddhas? First of all, we must understand the practice of the buddhas. The practice of the buddhas is carried on together with the whole world and with all sentient beings. If it is not a practice together with all things, it is not the practice of the buddhas. Therefore, from the time we first aspire to the Way until we attain enlightenment, both practice and attainment must be carried on with the whole world and all sentient beings."

Again, the "whole world and all sentient beings" does not infer spatial magnitude or number. Likewise, the attitude of the tenzo towards his work is one in which he "tries to build great temples from ordinary greens, which expounds the *buddhadharma* through the most trivial activity. . . . Handle even a single leaf of a green in such a way that it manifests the body of the Buddha. This in turn allows the Buddha to become manifest through the leaf."

To me, this is the fundamental spirit of Zen practice which has come down through the ages. In preparing even one cabbage leaf or burning one piece of wood, we must bring out the life that is contained therein.

Self, as the *buddhadharma*, means that everything we encounter is a part of our living body; neither the leaf of cabbage nor the piece of wood exist separately from us. Consequently, truly giving life to and bringing the best out of all aspects of our living body *is* giving expression to the life of the Self.

The *Tenzo Kyōkun* continues in detail concerning how we are to bring to life all the people and things we encounter in our life: "Cook the rice, soup, and any side dish all at the same time."

This one line may not mean much to intellectuals and white-collar executives, or to the old-fashioned householding chauvinists once prevalent in Japan who have little or no experience doing physical labor. But people who are used to working and to being conscientious about what they are doing should appreciate the profound meaning embedded in these words.

As I have mentioned over and over through these pages, life is neither something that can be neatly tucked away by numerical computation or logic and reason; nor is it a thing which responds to the touch of a button or the flip of a switch.

Even to prepare rice so that it turns out well, you have to know just how to cook and steam it. You cannot just add up the total number of calories of heat required and apply them blindly. *How* that heat is used is vital. Since this is not just some theoretical problem, but a dynamic life activity, we must not overlook the residual heat involved.

In general, it is said that all life on earth is the transformation of calories from the heat of the sun. Yet, obviously, if the earth were swallowed up by the sun all life would burn up in an instant. Everything alive lives within the residual heat of the sun, and precisely where this residual heat has steamed and ripened sufficiently, the highest form of life is born. This is something I feel we should deeply reflect upon.

When the tenzo cooks the rice, he has to carefully calculate the total amount of time required to both cook and steam the rice properly. When it comes to the soup, overboiling destroys the flavor and aroma of the miso, while leaving it sit too long after having brought it to a boil is no good either. You have to be especially careful if you put tofu in the soup, as overboiling kills the flavor of the tofu, while leaving the soup set for too long after removing it from the heat causes the same effect.

I remember reading a story about how one time Matsunaga Yasuzaemon was invited to a special ceremonial dinner before a formal tea ceremony at the home of Kobayashi Ichizō. When it was just about time for the soup course, Matsunaga began praising the soup beforehand, declaring what a pleasure it is to lift the lid off the soup bowl and see the steaming vapor waft upward. But when he actually took the lid off, the soup had already cooled and no vapor rose, so both Matsunaga, who had praised the soup prematurely, and Kobayashi, who was a poor host, were deeply embarrassed.

If the vapor had risen when the lid on the soup bowl was removed, undoubtedly everyone would have felt elated and gratified; however, that it did not work out that way goes to show a miscalculation on the part of both guest and host.

When you deal with calculations, it is only natural that there are going to be discrepancies; there is nothing that can be done about that. However, a tenzo who strives to bring out the fullest in life ought to think carefully about what he does, so that when the rice has been cooked and sufficiently steamed it can be brought into the *sōdō* at the same time the soup is ready. It is in this area, where the tenzo must use his ingenuity and creativity, that the practice of making vivid life calculations must be actualized.

TEN

Working with Clear Vision

In the previous discussion, I talked about life calculations. For a person working in the office of tenzo the most important calculation comes down to just what and how much is needed to prepare the meal.

"For every grain of rice to be eaten, supply one grain. In dividing one grain, the result may be two half-grains, or possibly three or four. On the other hand, one grain might equal a half-grain or perhaps two half-grains. Then again, two half-grains might be counted as one whole grain. You must be able to see clearly how much of a surplus will be created if you add one unit of rice, or whether there will be enough if you take away one unit.

"When you eat a grain of Luling rice you may become the monk Guishan. When you add a grain, you may become the cow. Sometimes the cow eats Guishan, sometimes Guishan pastures the cow!

"Consider whether you have thoroughly understood these matters and are able to make these calculations. Go back over everything again, and when you have understood these details be prepared to explain them to others according to their capacity to understand. Use ingenuity in your practice; see the cow and Guishan as one, not as two, even though temporarily they appear that way. In your day-to-day life, do not forget this even for a moment."

I have a feeling that there are many people who at first glance have no idea what Dōgen Zenji is talking about here. However, I have taken up this section deliberately so that we can see just how practical the *Tenzo Kyōkun* is and appreciate the close connection it has to our everyday lives.

In olden times, in China, the *saṃgha,* or practicing communities, were extremely large with sometimes 1,000 to 2,000 monks living together. Of course, they did not all live in the same hall. There would be various buildings and sub-temples scattered around the mountain. In addition to those practicing in the *sōdō* itself, where the main body of monks worked and practiced, there were undoubtedly many other people, such as priests who held the various offices, those in the sick room, and guests. In other words, there were many people with their own circumstances and situations spread out over the mountain. The tenzo's job must have been no easy task, keeping each one of these people in mind as he prepared the next meal.

As the numbers increase it becomes more and more difficult to fix everything so that there will not be much left over, and yet, be enough for everyone. Also, since monasteries depend upon offerings and donations, the tenzo simply is not in a position to throw away leftover food without batting an eyelash the way so many restaurants do today. He has to prepare just the right amount as skillfully as he can, which means he has to throw his whole life and mind into his work: "For every grain of rice to be eaten, supply one grain."

In general, it is only natural to think that if the number of people does not fluctuate too greatly you can figure out roughly how much gruel you will need for breakfast and about how much rice will be needed for the noon meal, or that you can calculate how much you will need by multiplying the amount one person will eat by the total number of people. That sort of rough estimation is not good enough. To make living calculations you have to be much more precise in your consideration.

For example, peoples' appetites vary with the seasons of the year. Also, everyone is bound to eat more if there is a special dinner being served and less at the following meal. If you think only in terms of preparing a set amount of food for every meal and fail to take these and other elements into account, you will invite disaster, since the amounts you have to deal with are so large.

Generally speaking, the amount a person eats in one day is fairly well fixed; if a big meal is served at noon then people are not likely to eat so much at the evening meal. Also, a person's salt intake does not normally vary too much, so if you cook a seasoned rice dish, you have to keep the soup lightly seasoned. The same applies to a soup served with noodles. If you season it lightly you have to make a lot, but if you season it heavily with salt and soy sauce you can get by with much less. Anyway, the total amount of salt used should be about the same. This is the meaning of the passage: "In dividing one grain, the result may be two half-grains."

Furthermore, when you are thinking about serving a variety of tempura, sweet potatoes, carrots, burdock, and lotus root you have to consider just how much of each of these you are going to need to fill one plate. Being just a little bit absent-minded, people who are not used to this work of the tenzo calculate the amount on the basis of how much they personally want to eat. They start thinking they want to eat five pieces of sweet potato tempura, and therefore, prepare five pieces for everyone. And everyone knows carrot tempura is good, so five pieces of that per person. Finally, since lotus root is their favorite—five pieces for everyone!

Now they have everything all cut up and ready for frying. They fry and fry until it seems like they will never be done. When they do finish they discover that they cannot fit five pieces of each onto one plate. So most of the tempura is left over and has to be eaten the next day, and perhaps the next as well. This sort of thing happens too often in monasteries because monks unaccustomed to the work all make the same mistake. What is important here is the succeeding passage: "In dividing one grain, the result may be two half-grains, or possibly three or four. On the other hand, one grain might equal a half-grain or perhaps two half-grains."

I cannot imagine housewives who are used to making these kinds of calculations making such foolish mistakes, but naturally this does not apply only to cooking. The other day I heard a story which further illuminates this point.

At one time, the area around Antai-ji was considered part of the extreme outskirts of Kyoto, but within the last few years it has been developing into a residential suburb, and fields that have been used for growing vegetables have become very valuable as building plots. One farmer in the neighborhood who had been farming for many years sold his fields for some ¥70,000,000 (well over $200,000 at that time). He had three young sons, so together with his wife there were five in the family. A problem arose when all five members of the family got carried away with the idea that they had seventy million yen. The farmer started going to a teahouse in Gion, which is Kyoto's traditional nightlife area, in a new car, and became a regular customer there. Everyday the children, each thinking they had seventy million yen to spend, visited the best bars and nightclubs along Kiyamachi, while the farmer's wife took in the department stores and theatres in the most expensive fashions available. Needless to say, the seventy million yen disappeared in no time. Each of them had made the mistake of thinking that they personally had seventy million yen, which, if it were the case, would have amounted to 350 million yen! Similar miscalculations can occur in company management and national politics, and could determine the fate of mankind. Calculations should be made with our eyes wide open and we should be aware of the ramifications of our choices. This is what lies behind the words of the above passage.

The calculations of the succeeding passage are equally important: "Then again, two half-grains might be counted as one whole grain." When you figure out what the total number of people who will be eating is, and count on each person consuming an equal amount, you are going to stumble into another type of miscalculation. Here you have to consider just who makes up the total number of persons eating. For example, you should add up the number of nuns, women, and old people, as well as the number of young monks who are apt to have a larger appetite. You should plan on the amount of food for the women and old people being likely to be about half of that required for the younger monks. Therefore, "Then again, two half-grains might be counted as one whole grain."

The text goes on: "You must be able to see clearly how much of a surplus will be created if you add one unit of rice, or whether there will be enough if you take away one unit."

In large monasteries, it is not permissible to run out of food, so you should prepare meals with a little extra in mind. You have to calculate the amount of rice and soup for the next meal inclusive of the existing leftovers, and in preparing the meal, you have to consider the margin that will be left over.

The above passage gives us a general idea of the sort of calculations the tenzo has to make. In spite of that, there is still a strong tendency to think that reasoning and using one's head have no place in Zen, and that Zen stories are a kind of directionless grasping at the clouds. Surely, it must be clear now that the refinements and subtleties of Dōgen Zenji's way of practice are not like that at all.[1] Far from it, making living calculations with your eyes open and continually being aware of the ramifications of your actions, using your intellect and yet seeing beyond just intellectual calculations is the ground of Dōgen Zenji's teaching. I believe the reason Dōgen brought up the kinds of examples that I quoted above concerning the rice, examples that are highly suggestive but difficult to penetrate at first reading, is because he was trying to show us that the decisions and distinctions we make in our lives go beyond the intellect, and that we must make them while being fully aware of their extensive consequences. As Dōgen's way of writing is difficult to fathom, I have picked out examples from my own personal experience as tenzo to explain them. Actually, my explanation is superfluous and may even cloud over the feeling of suggestion and subtle implication interwoven in Dōgen Zenji's teaching. I hope you will set my discussion aside and appreciate the *Tenzo Kyōkun* directly by reading it over and over. When working through it try to appreciate it not only as it relates to cooking, but as it relates to everything in your daily life. That means that you have to appreciate and learn from it and then draw on your own creativity to deepen your understanding and practice of it with regard to everyone you encounter in your life as well as all the situations and circumstances you might find yourself a part of.

"When you eat a grain of Luling rice, you may become the monk Guishan. When you add a grain, you may become the cow. Sometimes the cow eats Guishan, sometimes Guishan pastures the cow!"

The first thing to look at are these words "Luling rice," "Guishan," and "cow." There is an old story about Luling rice that goes like this. A monk asked Qingyuan Xingsi, "What is the essence of the *buddhadharma?*" Master Qingyuan replied, "What is the current price of rice in Luling?"

The *buddhadharma* is often expressed by the words *shogyō mujō*,[2] all things are impermanent. There is nothing we can point to as being fixed. On the other hand, if we become attached to the idea that everything is impermanent and nothing is fixed, then we have fallen into the trap of trying to fix something. Living out the dharma means to carry on our everyday activities seeing relatively fixed things where originally or fundamentally they are not so. At this juncture, it is important *not* to take it for granted that it is impossible to express the *buddhadharma* through language. It is essential that we express ourselves clearly and accurately whenever possible. Although there is really no way for me to resolve these old koans and stories by explaining them, I do so for the sake of clarification, and only as a tentative explanation.

The following story about Guishan and the cow has been passed down through the years: "One day Guishan said to the monks, 'A hundred years after my death, I will be reborn as a cow belonging to a parishioner near the skirt of this mountain. On the right flank of the cow will be written "I am Guishan." Now, if you say the cow is me, you are wrong because it is just a cow, and if you say it is just a cow, you are wrong because it will be me. So, what should you say?' "

This story by itself is a very intriguing one. However, if I had to break it down, this is the way I would go about it. Generally, we assume that what we call our "self" is some sort of fixed entity. Actually, though, there is no such fixed entity. Our metabolism is constantly changing and our consciousness is always flowing. What then would it be that we could call our "self"? There is no concrete entity like the stone inside a plum which we can call "I." And yet, though we say that nothing is fixed, it is not a matter of our "self" being nonexistent. As in the story of the Luling rice, our "self" occurs at the juncture of what is relatively fixed and what cannot be fixed. The practice of the *buddhadharma* is the attempt to express life *at that juncture* where that which is fixed intermingles with that which is indeterminate or undefined. For this reason it is difficult to understand. Through these stories in the *Tenzo Kyōkun* Dōgen Zenji tries to express a most subtle point about the expression and function of life.

In other words, "When you eat a grain of Luling rice you may become the monk Guishan." In a certain sense, we live by eating rice or whatever contains a certain amount of nutrition and which has a certain market price. At the same time, as we use our bodies to practice the Buddha's way of life, we give expression to the immeasurableness of the Buddha. But now, just eating rice does not guarantee that we are manifesting the infinity of the Buddha, for if we do not practice the Way, our bodies are just lumps of flesh. Or, we could look at it in the way the text puts it, "When you add a grain, you may become the cow."

What, then, is this body? Truly, it is neither an entity that is fixed, nor is it something undefined. If you eat food in order to do zazen, that is food for zazen. If you eat food in order to steal, it is just food for sustaining a thief. If you eat in order to go and sleep with a prostitute, it becomes rice for that purpose. To the extent that you do zazen with your body, "the cow eats Guishan."

You are mistaken if you think it is best to throw away your body (in this case, the cow) because you think it has no value, and just practice zazen (that is, Guishan). Our zazen becomes the *buddhadharma* precisely when it is functioning as *this* body in our *daily* life.

There will always be that complaining and unsatisfied aspect of the self with which we have to deal. The dharma is not going to become manifest only after we have somehow brought this aspect under control or stamped it out. The function of the dharma and of zazen is to care for the obstreperous aspect of ourselves in the same way a mother lulls her baby to sleep. In other words, "Guishan pastures the cow." I cannot help feeling that there is deep significance in the word "pasture."

Dōgen goes on to caution us concerning these matters: "Consider whether you have thoroughly understood these matters and are able to make these calculations. Go back over everything again, and when you have understood these details be prepared to explain them to others according to their capacity to understand. Use ingenuity in your practice."

Our discussion has taken quite a turn. Though the *Tenzo Kyōkun* is a text for the person in charge of preparing meals, you can see now that through this role, we can indeed practice and manifest the living dharma: "Use ingenuity in your practice; see the cow and Guishan *as one*, not *as two*, even though temporarily they appear that way. In your day-to-day life, do not forget this even for a moment."

In the original text, the expression *ichinyo*,[3] literally, "as one," refers to Buddha and all sentient beings, being as one. *Ninyo*, translated here "as two," means that they seem to be divided. That there is a separation between ourselves and the Buddha is not fixed. Tentatively the two appear as separate entities. Therein lies the reason we practice, aspiring to follow the Buddha's teachings. Yet, if you see the dharma as an entity separate from yourself, and make becoming a buddha the goal or object of your practice, you will be involved in a very fundamental mistake. The expressions *ichinyo* and *ninyo* will take on meaning only when you practice with the activities of a buddha as the direction of your work, and understand that the Buddha is not something separate from sentient beings, not something separate from yourself.

Finally, "in your day-to-day life, do not forget this even for a moment" implies that although practicing the dharma is something we do our whole life, the attitude of practicing right now, from day to day, in itself manifests eternity.

ELEVEN

Living Through the Life of the Self

To briefly summarize what I have been discussing so far, we have to live out our own lives, and we have to learn to encounter whatever comes up without avoiding difficulties. This is the spirit of magnanimity which Dōgen Zenji has referred to as *daishin,* or Big Mind. And, to meet all the experiences of our lives with our eyes open, and to act with a true sense of caring for them all is referred to as *rōshin,* or Parental Mind.

Dōgen Zenji wrote in elaborate detail about this spirit. Two of the examples he uses are taken from his travels in China. One concerns the tenzo from Mount Tiantong, and the other, the tenzo from Mount Ayuwang. Since these examples are rather lengthy I will not quote them here, but I recommend that you read them before reading over my commentary on them. These two stories appear on pages 9–11 of the text.

First of all, I would like to take up the discussion about the tenzo on Mount Tiantong. The core of this story centers around two passages: "Other people are not me" and "If I do not do it [my work] *now,* when else can I do it?"

I can best illustrate the attitude behind these passages by way of a letter I received recently from an old man who had been hospitalized and had to have someone write the letter for him. The man was suffering from paralysis of over half his body, and, in addition, had been rendered almost blind from cataracts. He wrote that in a very short time he would undoubtedly become totally blind and might even die. But, whenever he thought about death, he became dreadfully afraid. He no longer had any hope or joy in life and was completely bewildered as to how to cope with his situation.

77

What else can I say other than that his situation was truly a pitiable one. Yet, beyond that, what could I have possibly said or done for the man? What could I tell him that would have given him any comfort? The time is not too far off when I, too, will be in that or a similar condition, and then, who will come and suffer in my place?[1] Perhaps one of the postwar religions popular now might be able to assuage this man's fears for a brief period, but the emptiness of their promises would eventually drive him into a deeper despair from which he might very well never bound back.

The only thing that can be said for sure is that there is no possibility in life of exchanging even so much as a fart with another human being. Consequently, no matter what circumstances we fall into, we have no real choice but to live through it by ourselves. This absolute nature of life is something we must thoroughly recognize: "There is no way to gain emancipation through another." *(Suttanipāta: 773)*

"There is no way I can emancipate people suffering in this world. The only way for you to be able to cross over the stream of your passions is to know the highest truth of life." *(Suttanipāta: 1064)*

All too often people have grown so accustomed to living in a society of trade and compromise that even regarding their very own lives, they walk around in a fantasy world wondering if someone will come along to give them a hand. What else can we call this sort of suspension of reality other than fantasy?

The problem is that indulging in this sort of fantasizing is a way of avoiding the reality of the unfortunate circumstances that we have to deal with. At the same time, we develop a feeling that we are fighting a losing battle. Once we begin to wish that someone would come along to get us out of our mess, we start fantasizing all the more, and our situation looms even darker. Eventually things close in around us, causing us to begin to feel paranoid.

As difficult as it may seem to be, the highest, ultimate truth in life is grounded in the fact that there are no favorable or adverse circumstances, no fortune or misfortune. All there is, is the life of the Self.

A while back, I was riding on a train and overheard a discussion between two elderly businessmen sitting opposite me. One of them remarked that no one who possessed any of the following six characteristics would ever become a first-class businessman. These negative characteristics were opportunism, passivity, dependence upon others, arrogance, lack of concentration, and a tendency to swallow whole everything that people say without winnowing through it.[2] I made note of them because they do not apply only to business; they should be avoided in anything we do. These are all qualities antithetical to the stability of the Self. They are all a kind of turning outward, looking around for something good to show up. They are typical of an evasive posture that, after a while, we ourselves do not even notice. In taking such a posture, we confront the difficulties everyone has to face in life with a defeatist attitude.

When we thoroughly understand the attitude underlying these remarks made by the tenzo, "Other people are not me," and "If I do not do it *now*, when else can I do it," that is, when we understand that there is no stability to be found in life other than living it out as it is, we will be able to comprehend the reasoning behind the principle of becoming emancipated from our pain and suffering by just being resolved to living through it as it is.

I have been pursuing a life of *takuhatsu* (mendicant begging) for many years now.[3] On one occasion, in 1952, I was walking up the long hill of Takagamine toward Antai-ji, exhausted from the day's efforts. I kicked up a stone or a piece of glass in the dark and cut my toe. It was not much of a cut, so I paid it no mind other than to daub a little iodine on it when I got home. In a couple days a thin layer of skin formed over the cut, and I went out begging again without putting a bandage on it. It was raining that day and though the area around the cut got wet, I failed to clean it well when I got back to the temple. Skin formed around the cut although inside it began to fester and swell. Finally, the pain became worse and I developed a high fever.

It got so bad that I could no longer lie face-up because the pain from the toe went directly to my head. I piled up several quilts and laid on them. Though it was a cold November I could not stand clothing or blankets because of the fever and pain all through the left side of my body. I kept naked, cooling myself with the cold air, and suffered through this without a drop of sleep for three days and three nights. I frequently thought, well, if I am going to die then I will just die. But anyway, I was unable to see a doctor. Particularly during those days, the money I received from begging just would not have been enough to pay a doctor's bill. However, an elderly lady who lived nearby did bring me some licorice bulbs she had dug up and told me that if I ground them up, wrapped the mixture in paper, and applied it to my foot it would help bring down the fever. I did as she suggested, reapplying the dressing frequently. The following is something I wrote shortly after the incident:

Suffering a Foot Injury

If I had a wife to care for me,
if my parents were near,
if I had money,
I wouldn't have suffered.
In my dust-covered room
laying on ragged quilts
recalling Job—
"I can bear this hard pain"—
I am grateful.

People worry—
"what if I lose my savings,"
"what if I become ill,
lose my job?"
Always framing their thoughts
"what if . . ."
They're afraid, though their fears
are groundless.
Though I'm ill,
without savings,
or income,
unable to eat,
even if I starved
I wouldn't think it strange.
And just for that
I'm grateful.

November 1952

Through this experience I realized that when I stopped fighting the pain and just let it be inside of me, the burden of the suffering would be lifted. I have always felt this was an extremely valuable experience in my life. However, despite that, if I had to encounter such terrific pain again, I would only be fooling myself if I thought this past experience would be any help in breaking through the pain. Nothing ever occurs twice in life and the next time I encounter such pain there will be nothing for me to do but to live through it just as I did before. Or, it could be that the next time I will not be able to endure it. I may just give up and cry for help. But even then, the one certain thing is that the only person to live through the suffering will be me.

These passages, "Other people are not me," and "If I do not do it now, when shall I do it?" reflect an undeniable truth. The degree of separation from the reality of life appears as suffering and struggling. What we should be truly grateful for is that no matter how much we suffer and agonize, it is only suffering and agony going on in our minds, and when we die, this mind, too, passes away.

No matter what happens to us in our lives, there is no real alternative other than to live through it then and there, by ourselves—this is an inescapable reality![4] I cannot imagine anything more important in our lives than to completely resolve ourselves to the absolute nature of this truth.

TWELVE

On Life Force and Life Activity

Next, I would like to take up the section concerning the tenzo from Mount Ayuwang. As in the previous chapter, please read through the text itself before reading the commentary (pages 10–11 of the text.) The crux of this discussion centers around the *mondō*[1] and a succeeding *gāthā* of Xuedou which Dōgen Zenji brings up to clarify them. First of all, the *mondō* reads:

"I asked him once again, 'What are characters?'

" 'One, two, three, four, five [everything]' he replied.

" 'What is practice?'

" 'There is nothing in the world that is hidden [everything in your life is practice].' "

When he first arrived in China, Dōgen Zenji's attitude had derived from early Japanese Buddhism.[2] This attitude held Buddhism to be something special and mysterious, having no connection with ordinary people and their daily lives. At that particular time, Dōgen was not aware that the *buddhadharma* concerns religion as a force that, in a very practical way, guides the activities of everyday life.

Despite his old age, this monk from Mount Ayuwang was working very hard as a tenzo. Dōgen unthinkingly asked him: "But why, when you are so old, do you do the hard work of a tenzo? Why do you not spend your time practicing zazen or working on the kōans of former teachers? Is there something special to be gained from working particularly as a tenzo?"

The old monk just laughed at young Dōgen, because his query was so far off the mark. Being quite sensitive, Dōgen Zenji picked up on this and realized he had asked a rather foolish question. Feeling ashamed, he immediately asked what the meaning of characters and of practice is. To this the tenzo replied, "If you do not deceive yourself about this problem, you will be a man of the Way."

Dōgen Zenji, however, did not immediately understand the reply. On the other hand, the tenzo must have felt this young monk was an earnest student, since he did not simply let the matter drop, but he took the trouble to seek him out a few months later. This time, in response to the questions of the meaning of characters, the tenzo replied,

"One, two, three, four, five [everything]."

And, when Dōgen Zenji asked again about the meaning of practice, he replied, "There is nothing in the world that is hidden."

If I were to try to put this brief conversation into modern idiom I would do it this way. Dōgen Zenji asked, "What is the meaning of our day-to-day activities?"

The tenzo replied, "This and that—everything!"

Dōgen Zenji countered, "Just what is practice?"

The tenzo came back, "Everything you encounter in your life is your practice."

Next follows the *gāthā* of Xuedou:

> One, seven, three, five.
> The truth you search for cannot be grasped.
> As night advances, a bright moon
>   illuminates the whole ocean;
> The dragon's jewels are found in every wave.
> Looking for the moon, it is here,
>   in this wave, in the next.

The consistency between this *gāthā* and what the tenzo had talked of the previous year confirmed Dōgen Zenji's admiration of him as a true practitioner of the Way.

One way I could illustrate the meaning of this *gāthā* would be like this. I am not a scholar, nor am I that familiar with the particulars of this type of Chinese poetry. However, "One, seven, three, five" refers to one form of poetry which contains Chinese characters in the order of one, seven, three, and five per line.

As an example of this form, Sawaki Rōshi used to use the following poem:

1 *Sleeping*
7 (The) *moon's light shines* (through the) *window*
(like a) *bright silver coin.*
3 *No one thinks* (anything about it).
5 *Quietly* (the moon) *passes, shining* (its light)
near (one's) *pillow.*

There are many styles of poetry which use four lines of either five or seven characters per line. In the case of this particular *gāthā*, however, the standard form was ignored. In the original Chinese, the number of characters is completely different. This very unevenness or inconsistency with convention is the form our lives actually so often take. The things we encounter every day in our lives just do not arise in a smooth uniform order. Everything occurs in its own way—anything and everything arises! At least that would be a more realistic description of the "pattern" of our lives, if you want to call it a pattern.

In living this life day by day, in which anything might happen, we search for some absolute truth, but no matter how hard we try we never seem to be able to fix on anything solid that could be labeled "truth." The passage in the *gāthā* "it cannot be grasped" means that no matter how deep we search for something absolute to cling to, we will never find it. There is always that part of ourselves that wants to put its finger directly on some final universal truth. Life just is not that simple.

The next lines read, "As night advances, the bright moon illuminates the whole ocean; / The dragon's jewels are found in every wave." In this case, "jewels" refers to the reflection of the moon. "Looking for the moon, it is here, in this wave, in the next." In other words, the moon shines in all the waves of the ocean.

That is the gist of the *gāthā* as poetry, but now let us look at it from a different angle. Just what is Xuedou saying in this *gāthā?* As we live out our day-to-day lives, we encounter innumerable things and situations, and when we start to search for some sort of fixed truth we always fail. This is because the truth of life is only to be found "in this wave, in the next," that is, only in our *each and every* activity. Looking for the light of the moon, we find it in every wave.

Life is not a thing which is substantial or fixed; rather, it is our every activity. There is no way to see life outside of the vivid functioning of our every activity. For this reason, going back to the two earlier questions of the meaning of characters (our everyday life) and of practice, anyone who suggests that that meaning lies in some particular thing or in some special practice leads people astray. It is, as in the replies of the tenzo to Dōgen Zenji, "One, two, three, four, five."

From these passages I think it has become quite clear that the way in which our every activity must function is always here and now. Practicing the Buddha Way or practicing zazen is never a matter of putting aside our day-to-day activities to search for truth in some mystical realm, nor does it mean to look for truth through some scholarly research.

I have tried to point out through the earlier chapters what this means, and a little bit of what the *Tenzo Kyōkun* has taught me. However, if we are not very careful about this point, we are apt to be carried away by the belief that Zen practice is concerned with pursuing some state or condition that we have conjured up in our minds, or else to lose ourselves in some esoteric meditation practice. That kind of idle escapism or self-intoxication will never pass as the truth of life. Practicing the Way of the Buddha means to actually put our bodies to work, vividly living in every moment of our lives. I hope that from this we can finally learn within ourselves what practice truly is and what our attitude towards it ought to be.

In reading through the *Tenzo Kyōkun* in the original, you will come across words like *shōgon jōshin* or *seisei*, along with related expressions like *shishin* or *jōshin*, again and again. I have pretty much interpreted all these either as working with undivided attention or working with sincerity and without prejudice. The rationale behind this interpretation is that to actually function as human beings means to engage and work with our minds or spirits in objective situations. Yet, we are pulled by the tendency not to function with clear or undivided minds toward the true situation. We constantly run around fantasizing about our dissatisfactions and irritations, which only results in the vividness of our lives being clouded over; with muddled minds we encounter muddled and ambiguous situations.

Above everything else, the spirit running throughout the text is clearly that of functioning with a clear mind and true sincerity in the *actual* situation in which we find ourselves, and not in that one we have merely fabricated in our minds.

Returning to the words I cited above, I have rendered them in very conventional expressions. However, reading these ordinary expressions will not be adequate for comprehending the significance of the *buddhadharma*. What does "clear mind" or "true sincerity" or "actual situation" mean? This is where wordy explanations must leave off. Beyond this point you have to function in reality, to persevere and make every effort to study with both your body and your mind. This is your practice.

Returning to an earlier passage we looked at: "Both day and night, allow all things to come into and reside within your mind. Allow your mind (Self) and all things to function together as a whole". A few paragraphs later this passage continues: "These things are truly just a matter of course. Yet we remain unclear about them because our minds go racing about like horses running wild in the fields, while our emotions remain unmanageable, like monkeys swinging in the trees. If only we would step back to carefully reflect on the horse and monkey, our lives would naturally become one with our work. Doing so is the means whereby we turn things, even while simultaneously we are being turned by them."

By throwing our life force into our work, every situation literally comes to life and that in turn generates clarity and vividness. When the situation is full of life, we become more alive as a result. This means, then, that our life force has breathed a vividness into the situation. I feel very deeply that each of us must look clearly at this point for ourselves and then practice diligently with both our bodies and minds.

THIRTEEN

The Function of a Settled Life

The fundamental difference between Buddhism and other religions is that Buddhism has no God or gods before whom people bow down in return for peace of mind. The spirit enmeshed in the Buddha's teachings refuses to offer a god in exchange for freedom from anxiety. Instead, freedom from anxiety can only be found at that point where the Self settles naturally upon itself.

Beginning with Shakyamuni Buddha, the spirit reflected in the sutras was absolutely basic and unequivocal. Although I will not quote from the sutras here, the very early *Suttanipāta* and *Dhammapada*, both part of the Pali canon, or the Āgama sutras, will clarify this attitude. In reading through the sutras I am sure you will understand why "the Self settles naturally upon itself"[1] is the most fundamental teaching of Buddhism.

Far too often we get entangled in setting up some goal, and by pursuing that goal we invest it with the power to give meaning to our lives. Ironically, and unfortunately, we suffer because of our goals. Inflating a goal with great significance sets our "self" in opposition to the goal, and we suffer in direct proportion to our fixation with attaining the goal. Consequently, there is always going to be a sense of instability or anxiety in our lives.

Whatever goal we grab onto, accumulating money or credentials, gaining status, or having a family, can decline and fall apart. That way of life has no true stability. There is an interesting expression in Japanese that captures the sense of this: "One's goal and the Etchū *fundoshi* (loincloth) both part in front."[2] When doing zazen we practice ceasing to project some goal separate from the Self. Instead, we learn to live out completely that Self that settles upon itself. This is why

Dōgen Zenji writes that zazen is the standard or model of true peace and tranquility.³

Certain problems arise concerning this Self that employs zazen as a standard. When I use the term Self, I am not referring to some fixed entity; the Self is life, and life is functioning. Functioning means activity which works toward the world in which this Self lives. When I talk of a "Self settling upon itself," do not interpret this to mean a withdrawing and escaping from society. On the contrary, this expression means that your life manifests itself as life. It is a Self that works to settle or bring composure to everything you encounter in your life.

Without being dependent upon anything, and being willing to accept and face whatever comes up—this is the attitude of magnanimity, or in Japanese, *daishin*.⁴ Next, functioning with the attitude of a parent, seeing all the people and events we encounter in our lives as our children—this is what I referred to earlier as Parental Mind. In the text, this is referred to as *rōshin*.

Taking the discussion one step further, discovering the true meaning of our lives through this parental attitude is called *kishin,* or Joyful Mind. In the *Tenzo Kyōkun*, Big Mind, Parental Mind, and Joyful Mind are called the "three minds."

The teaching of the *Tenzo Kyōkun* is, through our practice of preparing meals, to develop these attitudes in order that they become integrated into the way we live out all the aspects of our lives. For this reason, the role of the tenzo in the *saṃgha* provides us with a tremendous opportunity for practice. Merely to study Buddhist thought and philosophy through books, or to do zazen only to become entranced by satori as some rapturous and esoteric state of mind without actually putting our bodies to work in our day-to-day lives as taught in our text, leaves grave doubts as to whether we have any idea at all of what it means to truly live out the *buddhadharma*.

The following passage concerns the spirit of joy: "The Joyful Mind is one of gratefulness and buoyancy. You should consider this carefully. If you had been born into some heavenly realm, you would most likely have only become attached to the pleasures of that realm, taking neither time nor opportunity to awaken the *bodhi*-spirit, nor would you likely feel any particular necessity for practicing the *buddhadharma*. Much less would you be able to prepare meals for the Three Treasures despite their being the highest and most worthy of all things. Neither being Śakro-devānām-indraḥ nor a *cakravartin* compares with the Three Treasures.

"In the *Chanyuan Qinggui* we find this passage: 'The *saṃgha* is the most precious of all things. Those who live in this community are unfettered by the pettiness of social affairs. Such a community manifests a refined posture devoid of fabrication about the world.'

"How fortunate we are to have been born as human beings given the opportunity to prepare meals for the Three Treasures. Our attitude should truly be one of joy and gratefulness.

"We should also reflect upon what our lives might have been had we been born in one of the realms of hell, as an insatiable spirit, as some lowly animal, or as a demon. How difficult our lives would be if we suffered the misfortunes of these four circumstances or any other of the eight misfortunate conditions. We would be unable to practice the dharma with the strength of the community even though we had a mind to do so. Much less would we be able to prepare food with our own hands and offer it to the Three Treasures. Our bodies and minds would be bound by the limitations and afflictions of those worlds and have to suffer their burdens.

"Therefore, rejoice in your birth into the world, where you are capable of using your body freely to offer food to the Three Treasures: the Buddha, the Dharma, and the *Saṃgha*. Considering the innumerable possibilities in a timeless universe we have been given a marvelous opportunity. The merit of working as a tenzo will never decay. My sincerest desire is that you exhaust all the strength and effort of all your lives—past, present, and future—and every moment of every day into your practice through the work of the tenzo, so that you form a strong connection with the *buddhadharma*. To view all things with this attitude is called Joyful Mind.

"The deeds of even a benevolent ruler disappear quickly like foam on water or the windblown flame of a candle. Rather than be as such a ruler, it would be of more value to the *buddhadharma* for you to prepare and offer meals to the Three Treasures."

I did not learn about the *Tenzo Kyōkun* nor about Joyful Mind until after I became a monk. I can still recall how moved I was the first time I read this passage and how much I wanted to work as a tenzo as soon as the opportunity arose.

As I mentioned earlier, I did not get to do so until after I came to Antai-ji in 1949, where I served as tenzo for sixteen years until the death of Sawaki Rōshi in 1965. A small *saṃgha* like ours presented its own difficulties for a tenzo, such as keeping a continuous supply of pickles, fresh vegetables, and firewood throughout the year, in spite of the frequent fluctuations in the number of people coming in and out of the temple. I had to do all the sawing and wood-splitting, in addition to the farming and pickling, all by myself. Yet, thanks to the strength that I gained from this passage on Joyful Mind, I was able to throw myself into the work even though I was already well into my forties. I shall always be grateful for this.

It seems to me that to really understand Dōgen Zenji's remarks on Joyful Mind, we have to begin by asking ourselves in just what direction our lives are heading—what are we trying to do with our lives, and what should we really be doing.

Spending our lives chasing after money, fame, or the growth and success of our children, goals that "disappear quickly like foam on water or the windblown flame of a candle"—that is a meaningless life.

What should we be doing with our lives? Sawaki Rōshi always said that we need to learn what it means to emerge from a life which is confused, incomplete, and carelessly haphazard, a life based on compromise, on always fooling ourselves and others about who we are, about how we live; we need to learn what it means to "settle naturally into our lives."

We spend too much of our time living only by force of habit, or by trying to escape from boredom, or by throwing our energies in some fanatical direction completely opposite from living in as fundamental a way as possible. Now more than in any age before, though we cannot spend all our time pondering every little thing, we do need to take time out to reflect seriously on the significance of settling our lives. This expression of Sawaki Rōshi's on settling our lives is his way of explaining a passage found in the chapter entitled *Kie Bupposō-hō* (Having Faith in the Three Treasures) of the *Shōbō-genzō*. It says: "Why should we have faith in the Three Treasures?" And the reply is: "Because the Three Treasures are one's final refuge."[5]

In other words, we have faith in Buddhism, and by Buddhism, I mean the trinity of the Buddha, the Dharma, and the *Saṃgha,* since it shows us the way of an ultimately settled life. In spite of that, people think nothing of standing in line all night to get tickets for a special football game or musical stage show, packing together like sardines to watch it, while on the other hand they fall asleep when they hear someone talk about a settled way of life, the very way of life constantly referred to throughout the sutras. Dōgen Zenji tries to express this idea in the following passage: "If you had been born into some heavenly realm, you would most likely have only become attached to the pleasures of that realm, taking neither time nor opportunity to awaken the *bodhi*-spirit, nor would you likely feel any particular necessity for practicing the *buddhadharma*."

In this age of leisure time and luxuries where the vast majority of people, at least those in industrialized countries, are immersed in one heavenly realm or another, perhaps it is natural for there to be a tremendous distance between oneself and any aspiration to practice such an ordinary but genuine and steady way of life as found in Buddhism. Yet, it is in just such an age that far from going out, the light of the Three Treasures, which illuminates the true significance of a settled life, is needed all the more.

Those who are determined to live out this style of life and center themselves around a practice of zazen are real living buddhas. Hence, the following passage from the *Chanyuan Qinggui*: "The *saṃgha* is the most precious of all things. Those who live in this community are unfettered by the pettiness of social affairs. Such a community manifests a refined posture devoid of fabrication about the world."

The tenzo's function is to prepare meals for the Three Treasures, furnishing these living buddhas with the appropriate nourishment to enable them to become people grounded in zazen. Can there be any human endeavor superior to this? Whether one is a king, a president, a prime minister, or a chairman of a party, Dōgen Zenji writes that not to experience working as a tenzo is to waste one's life away. Over the years, I, too, have come to feel the same way about this.

To achieve a Joyful Mind, then, is first to become clearly aware of the significance of the function of the tenzo and then to pour all your life energy into the work itself. To talk of such a spirit of joy is totally different from simply feeling happy. It has no connection with the ecstasy lovers might feel entwined in each others' arms, or the tears of joy at being converted to some new religion. Functioning as a tenzo is just hard, and at times, painful work. There is no time to get enraptured in religious ecstasy. Yet, throwing all your passion for life into that work—that is what it means to have a Joyful Mind.

FOURTEEN

Throwing Your Life
into the Abode of the Buddha

One time after a three-day *sesshin*,[1] as we were all having tea together, someone asked me what I did for fun. It was a totally unexpected question for me, since the sort of life I have been living precludes having much fun.

First of all, we have a five-day *sesshin* each month at Antai-ji. There is no talking allowed during this period and your legs only hurt more with each day. When it is over, the only relief is the knowledge that you have been able to somehow get through another one. Then, in the middle of each month, I usually leave the temple for a few days for another *sesshin* somewhere. At the *sesshin* outside Antai-ji we only sit about seven or eight hours a day, but I still have to give dharma-lectures twice a day, and in addition to that, during any rest time I receive guests who would not normally be able to visit Antai-ji.

When I am not involved in one *sesshin* or another, I try to catch up on correspondence that comes into the temple or else receive guests. On top of all this, I spend as much time as I can with my disciples, plus do some reading and work with various manuscripts.

So, somehow, the word "fun" is not exactly the way I would describe my activities.

Anyway, I suddenly recalled one thing I do which you might call fun, and that is sipping three small shots of whiskey after the day's work is done and I am alone in my room looking at some book on animals or other light material. Personally, I do not care much for alcohol and cannot stand sitting around drinking with a bunch of people. The reason I drink is because even after I have been in bed for some time my feet never seem to get warm, so several years back

I decided to try getting warm from the inside by taking a couple shots of whiskey. The life we lead here at Antai-ji, however, is far from the kind that allows the sipping of hot sakè and the nibbling of snacks with it. I drink with the express purpose of warming my feet, and have grown accustomed to taking the whiskey straight to maximize its effect. The light reading serves as my drinking partner and snack. Now, if the word "fun" could be applied to this situation, then this is the time I have fun.

At the same time, I added that I do not live my life to have fun. The way I experience the meaning and value of my life is by throwing all my passion for living into everything I do. I am afraid that if having pleasure were the purpose of my life, then three shots of whiskey a day would be it. And, if I were to take that seriously, how could I help but think that I live anything but a pretty wretched existence. It is vital here when talking about the meaning of life to clearly distinguish between emotional feelings of pleasure or joy and devoting oneself to that passion for life.

When people complain of being unhappy and of living a meaningless or empty life, I wonder if it is not because they have taken it for granted that the meaning of their life is to be found simply in some sort of emotional pleasure or joy. If you decide that only this sort of "happiness" constitutes the meaning of your life, then it only follows that you are going to feel a hollowness in what you do, for there is just no such thing as never-ending pleasure or happiness.

I would like to take another look at what it means to have a passion for life. Normally we waste our whole lives playing with toys. As I described briefly in *Approach to Zen,* the first toy people clamor for when they are born is their mother's breast. Then, it is on to teddy bears and electric trains, and as we get older, bicycles, watches, cameras, and finally, jewelry, clothes, and the opposite sex.

When you consider things carefully, it seems that we have a tendency to fill our whole lives with toys, trying to make sense out of our lives only in relation to these toys. In this respect, I cannot help but feel that a lot of scholarly study and research and all of one's trying to get rich in business is just so much playing with toys. The same goes for the attitude of competing with the Joneses as well as other forms of social climbing. As men reach their forties and their sexual drive begins to fade, fame suddenly rises up to become the most interesting toy. People throw all their energies into becoming the best in their fields.

In Japan these days women around that age often center their lives on spurring their children on in their studies in order to get them into the best university or the best company.

Finally, in their old age, people busy themselves with collecting antiques, attending various tea-ceremony functions, or visiting temples.[2] In other words, with the same mentality as children, people while away their whole lives over some toy or another. I suppose you could add to this list of toys most of the superzealous religions that have become popular since World War II.

Essentially, what is the difference between rich widows crowding around some famous priest or guru and teenage girls clamoring after some rock star? Where do you differentiate between getting drunk on alcohol or becoming fanatic over some "born again" religious experience?

Earlier, I tried to differentiate between seeking meaning in terms of emotional happiness and of just devoting your passion for life. To carry the discussion a step further, we have to examine closely just where this passion for life is actually being devoted. Throwing one's energies into the pursuit of fame appears to be a meaningful way for a person to spend life, although, fundamentally, it is nothing more than another link in the chain of playing with toys.

In Buddhism, finding the meaning of life never means to search for it among toys. A life which relies on toys for its value means nothing more than that one is being led around by those toys, thus losing sight of living with true purpose or intensity. To live the *buddhadharma* is to live without the necessity of having to be constantly entertained by toys. Having a passion for life means only to pour all our life forces into your true Self. Life, in terms of everything we encounter, the people with whom we come into contact, all the material things we use and handle every day—*that* is our life and our true Self, and it is into this that we throw our life force.

In the *Shōji* (Life and Death) chapter of the *Shōbō-genzō*, Dōgen Zenji takes up the problem of the relationship between life and death. In a sense, this chapter is a condensation of all of his teachings. The following passage represents the essence of that chapter: "Let go of and forget your body and mind; throw your life into the abode of the Buddha, living by being moved and led by the Buddha. When you do this without relying on your own physical or mental power, you become released from both life and death and become a buddha.

Do not immerse yourself in mental and emotional struggles. Refrain from committing evil. Neither be attached to life nor to death. Be compassionate toward all sentient beings. Revere that which is superior and do not withold sympathy from that which is inferior. Do not harbor hatreds nor covet anything. Do not be overly concerned with trivial matters nor grieve over difficulties in your life. This is the Buddha. Do not search for the Buddha anywhere else."

When I first read this passage while I was a student, I felt a very strong resistance to it. For example, I thought that "Revere that which is superior and do not withhold sympathy from that which is inferior" meant to respect the wealthy and pity the poor, or perhaps to defer to those in high positions and be paternalistic towards those in low ones. For a while, I began to think that Dōgen Zenji was no more than another member of the aristocracy in an age when class distinctions were strictly observed. However, the years have changed my understanding. I do not see people with money nor those who are in high positions as being superior, nor do I view people as inferior simply because they are materially poor and hold no particular position.

Although I no longer see this passage the way I did when younger, I have come to see that there is superior and inferior, but in a completely different sense. I think that spiritual teachers who have genuinely striven to develop and refine their lives and the life of the world around them, in addition to those who have years of rich experiences and are willing to share them with others, ought to be revered. On the other hand, we cannot but be naturally sympathetic and understanding towards the sick and the aged who are no longer able to get around for themselves as they could when they were younger. I do not believe as I once did that everything ought to be equal (mistakenly thought to be synonymous with "same"). To talk of dividing the wealth and daily necessities of the Earth equally among all people sounds too hollow or abstract when you consider the tremendous differences in the life styles and life needs of the Eskimos and the South Sea Islanders.

Returning again to the *Tenzo Kyōkun,* we find the passage: "Put those things that naturally go on a high place onto a high place, and those that would be most stable on a low place onto a low place; things that naturally belong on a high place settle best on a high place, while those things which belong on a low place find their greatest stability there."

If there is anything which we should aim for through our work, it must be this: to ensure that those things that belong on a high place and those things that belong in a low place are stable as they are.

Although the problem of superior and inferior was resolved for me there still remained, in a religious sense, a more serious problem. In *Shōji*, the opening lines, which I quoted above, read, "Let go of and forget your body and mind, throw your life into the abode of the Buddha, living by being moved and led by the Buddha." As a young man, I could never figure out just what "the abode of the Buddha" was supposed to mean. If there is some special kind of Buddhist life style into which we throw our bodies and minds, then it would seem logical to assume that there must be some power within ourselves to do this, and that this power would have to derive from a practice based upon personal power, or in Japanese, *jiriki*. If I had had such a power within myself, there would never have been any necessity to suffer as I had. This was a big problem for me.

When I look back upon it now, it seems to me that the error in my thinking was to assume that there existed some sort of "place" separate from myself into which I had to throw my body and mind. Actually, however, the "abode of the Buddha" is nothing other than our own lives. Consequently, there is no refuge, no special place outside the life of our true Self, nor anything apart from the activities of that Self.

In the *Tenzo Kyōkun*, it is expressed this way: "Be very clear about this. A fool sees himself as another, but a wise man sees others as himself."

The true Self includes the entire world in which it lives. Therefore, there is nothing that is not a part of it. Everything encountered is life. To devote ourselves to everything we encounter and throw our life force into doing just that is quite different from simply exhausting our energies playing with toys. Here is where our passion for life as Joyful Mind manifests the significance of being alive.

In tying this text together, there is one more point I would like to make concerning the life of the *buddhadharma*. It is a point which I feel is most essential and practical. During his last few years, there was an expression Sawaki Rōshi used and emphasized a great deal: "Gain is delusion; loss is enlightenment." As I have mentioned in various ways throughout this commentary, the way of life of one living the *buddhadharma* is, at the most fundamental level, just living the life of the Self without searching outside oneself for something. Consequently, there is no exchanging back and forth with others. In this sense, "no gain, no loss, no enlightenment, no delusion."[3] And yet, ordinarily, we spend our lives thinking this amalgamation of skin and bones is the Self, and constantly run around holding it up and comparing it with others. In our daily lives, if we live fully aware of the most fundamental reality, which is that our lives are everything we encounter, that everything which befalls us is our true Self, then it has to become obvious that, practically speaking, gaining is delusion and losing is enlightenment. For us to make an effort not to pile up material or social possessions—money, riches, or fame—is enlightenment, and this effort becomes the foundation of our practice. I have always held these words to be the practical principle of Sawaki Rōshi's teachings, and have striven in whatever meager way possible to carry them out.

This same attitude is reflected in the *Tenzo Kyōkun* in the following two passages: "You should think only about how to best serve the community, having no fear of poverty. As long as your mind is not limited, you will naturally receive unlimited fortune"; and "The three aspects of this attitude are to see that working for the benefit of others benefits oneself; to understand that through making every effort for the prosperity of the community one revitalizes one's own character; and to know that endeavoring to succeed and to surpass the patriarchs of past generations means to learn from their lives and to value their examples."

Indeed, this is the fundamental spirit or attitude of the bodhisattvas, who vow to actually practice not for their own benefit alone but for the benefit of all sentient beings.

Notes

On the Tenzo Kyōkun

1. Buddha's Way, in Japanese, *butsudō*. More than anything else, living out one's life in the Buddha's Way means to live constantly *settling* one's life. In the chapter entitled *Kie Buppōsō-hō* (Having Faith in the Three Treasures) of the *Shōbō-genzō* it says: "Why should we have faith in the Three Treasures?" The reply, "Because the Three Treasures are one's final refuge, enabling human beings to go beyond birth and death, and realize great enlightenment." (This passage was translated from the *Kōhon Kōtei Shōbō-genzō*, published by Chikuma Shobō and edited by Ōkubo Dōshū, in 1971. Further explanation concerning this passage can be found in chapter 12 of the commentary.)

2. The six offices (or officers) are *tsūsu*, and *kansu*, in charge of the overall affairs of the community; *fūsu*, in charge of financial and clerical affairs; *ino*, in charge of personal affairs within the community; *tenzo*, in charge of meals and food supplies; and *shissui*, in charge of building repairs, farming, and other work.

3. "activities of a buddha," in Japanese, *butsuji*. To carry out buddha activities means to actually put your life to work, that is, to make it function, in a way that things become most settled.

4. The *Chanyuan Qinggui* (Regulations

for Zen Monasteries) or in Japanese, *Zen'en Shingi*, consists of 10 volumes of the oldest existing regulations for running a monastery. They were written by Zongze of Mount Zhanglu, in A.D. 1102. In Japanese he is known as Chōro Sōsaku, that is, Sōsaku of Mount Chōro.

5. In the original, the expression *bendō* is used. The character *ben* has two possible nuances, one meaning to discriminate or discern, and the other, to make an effort or exert one's energies. Though Dōgen Zenji probably means to imply both, in this particular case, the latter meaning is being stressed: to throw one's energies into pursuit of the Buddha's Way of life.

6. The text uses the expression *dōshin*, literally, "way-seeking mind." Uchiyama Rōshi defines this in modern idiom as having the mind or attitude that seeks to manifest here and in every moment, the highest or most refined life of the Self. Lest the reader misinterpret the word refined, which will appear frequently throughout this book, in terms of some sort of aristocratic or leisure-class refinement, I would like to include a passage from Dōgen Zenji which Uchiyama Rōshi quoted in his own book *Jiko* (Self), published by Hakujusha Publishers, Tokyo, 1965:

"I don't want to suggest that there is anything inherently virtuous about being poor. What I'm saying is that I am thankful for having been able to pursue the highest form of culture, that is, just doing zazen, despite being materially poor. Dōgen Zenji himself wrote, 'Pursuing the most refined culture within a life of poverty is the most valuable pursuit we can undertake in this world.' To the extent that I have been able, I have taken these words as the ideal mode of living for my life."

In Uchiyama Rōshi's translation, after "lacks such spirit" there is an added phrase "and is indifferent about his life." The word *dōshin* has two aspects. One involves the concept that originally or fundamentally we are already fully awakened or complete, and the other, that we must pursue a continual or ongoing seeking of the Way. In our day-to-day activities it is meaningless to simply say that we are awakened unless we practice that awakened condition through *each* of our activities. This dual aspect of our being awake is explained thoroughly in the *Daijō Kishin Ron* (The Awakening of Faith), and is also the point that Dōgen Zenji is making in the example of the monk and Hōtetsu concerning the fan and the wind. It is not enough to know that the *wind's* nature is to be everywhere (enlightenment). We must also practice that enlightenment (use the fan). (This example is in the *Shōbō-genzō: Genjō Kōan*.)

7. "Buddhas and patriarchs." This expression derives from the word *busso*. Historically, it refers to the buddhas in India and the lineage of patriarchs in China. However, there is another way to interpret this word that is equally valid and theologically much more important; that is as buddha-patriarchs. In other words, buddhas do not exist apart from patriarchs.

Another nuance of this compound is that the word buddha connotes completeness or absoluteness, while the word patriarch has a more dynamic, developing, or relative ring to it.

8. Uchiyama Rōshi translates the Japanese expression *udō* as "those who have sought to live out their lives in the most settled way."

9. In olden times, only two meals a day were served in the monasteries.

10. This is a large room or hall (*shuryō*) used by the community for study or having tea.

11. "Put your undivided attention into the work" is an interpretive translation of the expression *shōgon jōshin*, while "seeing just what the situation calls for" refers to the expression *makoto*, that is, the true situation seen without prejudice.

Dōgen Zenji's use of *shōgon jōshin* and similar expressions referring to the attitude or spirit of the practitioner include both a sense of "undividedness" or concentration in every situation, as well as an attitude of sincerity and of working without prejudice.

12. In Uchiyama Rōshi's modern-day translation he includes an extra sentence to clarify the above passage. It reads "A great ocean is made up of many drops of water and a high mountain from many particles of sand."

The Japanese expression for "source of goodness" is *zengon*. *Zengon* means the meritorious power of good deeds. It is the influence or power which increases good. "Good is defined as that which follows in accord with dharma, or that which follows in accord with the essence of truth or suchness, *shinnyo*, and which is beneficial to all beings in all worlds as peace or tranquility. In the *Daibibasharon* (*Abhidharma-mahāvibhāṣā-śāstra*) it is written, "Just as leaves and branches flow from the roots of trees, good grows from the power of the life force."

(The above passage was taken from the *Zengaku Dai Jiten* compiled at Komazawa University and published by Daishūkan Shoten in 1978.)

13. The six flavors are bitter, sour, sweet, salty, mild, and hot. The three virtues are light and flexible, clean and neat, conscientious and thorough.

In Japanese, the three virtues are called *kyōnan, jōketsu,* and *nyohō.* The latter word, *nyohō,* generally has three meanings; first, everything that exists, that is, all things and phenomena; second, the natural laws that apply to all phenomena that exist; and third, the *buddhadharma,* that is, the composed or settled activity that works towards greater composure and stability. Here, the expression includes all three meanings. That is, all things functioning as they naturally do in accord with the natural laws and settling towards greater stability is *nyohō.*

14. In this case, "rice" and "sand" are being used metaphorically to represent right views and mistaken views, or perhaps wisdom and enlightenment, as opposed to illusions and desires.

15. Dongshan is not questioning the act of turning over the pot as an expression of Xuefeng's understanding. It is simply that for Dongshan the act was a bit overdramatic. Xuefeng did eventually study under another master, Deshan who was famous for his more demonstrative approach. Later on, these differences in style led to the dual flowering of the Rinzai and Sōtō schools.

16. The original text is unclear concerning the order in which the tasks should be performed resulting in various translations of the first few lines of this passage. I have translated those lines in what I feel would be the most logical order for doing them.

The passage which begins, "Put those things that naturally go on a high place..." is a quotation Dōgen Zenji took from a story about Guishan Lingyou and Yanshan Huiji. The story reads as follows:

"One day Guishan and Yanshan went to make a new rice paddy. Yangshan said, 'It's pretty low here and rather high over there, isn't it?' Guishan replied, 'We can measure the level with water.' Yangshan rebutted, 'We can't depend upon water as a standard, Master! A high place is level as a high place and a low place is level as a low one.' "

17. A *kamado* is a wood-burning stove made of adobe, stones, or bricks, used for cooking in both China and Japan.

18. In the *Chanyuan Qinggui,* the *kusu* is referred to as the officer of the overall affairs of the community. Later on, this office was shared by three officers, the *tsūsu, kansu,* and *fūsu.* The three officers together were then designated as the *kusu.*

19. Uchiyama Rōshi's modern translation reads, "Both day and night everything we encounter is our life. Because of that, we put our life into everything we encounter. Our life and what is being encountered become one. We exhaust our life force so that our life and encounter might function as they should."

The above passage does seem circular, and, in fact, in this respect it is; that when we throw ourselves into our work, there ceases to be a "gap" or duality between our life force and the "thing" or "work" which is being encountered, so that the opposing meanings of all the ordinarily dualistic words— "our," "life," or "force" on the one side, and "thing" or "work" on the other—fall away.

20. In Uchiyama Rōshi's translation, he adds that we must not lose sight of this spirit.

21. For clarification, Uchiyama Rōshi adds, "We must aspire to the highest of ideals, yet remain humble in our manner." This sentence does not appear in the original.

22. A similar passage can be found in *Gakudō Yōjinshū* (Points to Watch in Practicing Buddhism): "When practicing the Way, from the very beginning, listen to the teacher and conduct your self in accordance with his teaching. You should remember and know thoroughly that dharma turns the Self [all phenomena influence us] and that the self turns dharma [we influence all

dharma or phenomena]. When we in-fluence dharma, dharma is weak and we are strong. When dharma influences us, dharma is strong and we are weak. Both of these principles have always been a part of the Teachings of the *buddhadharma*."

23. Uchiyama Rōshi's translation reads: "Even when handling just one leaf of a green, do so in such a way that the leaf manifests the fullness of its potential, which in turn, allows the illumination of buddha to radiate through it. This is a power of functioning whose nature is incapable of being grasped with the rational mind and one which operates without hindrance in a most natural way. At the same time, this power operates in our lives to clarify and settle activities beneficial to all living things."

24. The *sōdō* is the main hall or build-ing in which the monks of the monas-tery carry on their practice. Sleeping, eating, and zazen are traditionally carried on in the *sōdō*.

25. Luling is a district in China, although in this case, it is an indirect reference to an old story in which Luling rice is mentioned. Refer to chap-ter 10 for more details.

26. The *kesa* is the outermost robe worn by a priest. It is a symbol of the robe that Shakyamuni wore, and is usually worn over the left shoulder and under the right one.

27. The *zagu* is a square piece of cloth which is spread out on the ground or floor. The priest either sits on top of it or does prostrations, depending upon what the situation calls for.

28. This passage is an interpretive translation of the Japanese expressions *taiho honshin* and *anraku*. *Taiho* means to step back, that is to refrain from making emotional or prejudiced judgments, while *honshin* means to move one's body in an animated way, in other words, to put your body to work. *Anraku* implies not fantasizing either in one's head or

with one's body. *Anraku* is also the Chinese translation for the Sanskrit word *nirvāṇa*.

29. The *butsuden* is one of the buildings or large halls in which a statue of a buddha or bodhisattva is enshrined.

30. "I spent my time in total confusion as to what I was doing." This passage should be understood as an expression of modesty on the part of the monk.

31. The "summer practice period" or *natsu ango* officially runs in most Zen monasteries from around April 19th to July 15th.

32. May 5th is one of the festival days celebrating the change in seasons.

33. "The practice of an old man." Again, this is simply an expression of humility on the part of the monk.

34. Koans are rationally unsolveable problems consisting of stories or com-ments made by past teachers. In the Rinzai tradition, the teacher gives a koan to the student to work on during zazen. For Dōgen Zenji, however, the connotations and implications of the word are much broader. More can be read about this in the chapter *Genjō Kōan* of the *Shōbō-genzō*.

35. "the meaning of characters." The tenzo is, of course using the word char-acters, or in Japanese, *monji*, to mean the written word, although in a broader sense he is referring to all phenomena as well.

36. Uchiyama Rōshi translates this passage, "If you understand precisely what you're asking to be the most vital problem concerning the *buddhadharma*, then *that* in itself is understanding char-acters, *that* is practice."

37. "There is nothing in the world that is hidden." This is derived from the expression *hengai fuzōzō*, meaning that the truth of life manifests itself in all places and in all things, just as they are. When the tenzo counts to five, he implies that "everything" is the answer; here he says that everything in our lives is practice.

38. Myōzen was a senior disciple of Eisai Zenji, when the latter was abbot at Kennin-ji in Kyoto. Historically, it is unclear as to whether Dōgen actually met Eisai Zenji or not. In either event, Dōgen Zenji did study several years with Myōzen before accompanying him to China. Myōzen died while in China at the age of 42.

39. *Gāthā*, or *ju* in Japanese, are poems extolling the *buddhadharma*. Xuedou Zongxian, A.D. 980–1052, was a Song-Dynasty Zen master famous for his poetry, which was later compiled and commented on by Yuanwu Keqin. The poetry and commentaries are known as the *Blue Cliff Records*.

40. "6, 7, 8, 9, and 10." That is, though the phenomena we encounter before and after enlightenment are the same, the function completely changes.

41. Genuine Zen is a translation of Dōgen Zenji's expression *ichimi zen*, which means literally, "one-flavor Zen." That is, Zen which is unadulterated by limited views. *Ichimi zen* is being used in contrast to *gomi zen*, literally, "five-flavor Zen," which I translated as "variously tainted Zen." In other words, *ichimi zen* is Zen which is untainted by various types of humanistic or altruistic motives.

Uchiyama Rōshi translates this passage as follows: "If you practice in this manner, you will be able to grasp Zen as incomparable life in its widest dimensions, that goes beyond the surface of characters. Otherwise, you will be hindered by *gomi zen* that has been tainted by various rankings and which is being practiced here and there, causing you to lose sight of life that is vigorous. Consequently, even when preparing meals for the community, you will be unable to function with the utmost intensity."

42. It is said that whenever Shakyamuni gave discourses on the *buddhadharma* he constantly emitted a ray of light called the *byakugōkō*. This ray was emitted from between his eyebrows. Dharma descend-

ants in later ages (including our own) live thanks to this light.

43. This story appears in part 8 of the *Daichidoron*, in Sanskrit, *Mahāprajñāpāramitopadeśa*.

44. This story appears in section 5 of the *Ayuwang Jing* (The Sutra of King Asoka).

45. This saying is found in the *Soeishū*, a text of the Tendai School of Buddhism, in which Dōgen Zenji first studied. In this text, Katyayana Sonja accepted an invitation to eat with a certain king. However, the king, in addition to serving several fine delicacies also offered a number of ordinary dishes. Katyayana Sonja showed no special delight at the delicacies nor aversion towards the more common dishes. The king could finally take it no longer and asked Katyayana why he behaved that way. Katyayana replied, "The mouth of a monk is like an oven. Just as an oven burns both sandalwood [incense] and cow dung [for cooking] without distinction, our mouths should be the same. There should be no distinction between delicious food and food which is plain and simple. We should be satisfied with whatever we receive."

46. "Incomparable wisdom." This is a translation of the Sanskrit expression *anuttara-samyak-sambodhi*, which means unexcelled, supreme, hence, incomparable wisdom of enlightenment.

Uchiyama Rōshi translates this passage as follows: "Since a monk should have the aspiration to practice directly the functioning of *anuttara-samyaksambodhi*, which means the most refined or stable way of life, even if there is right or wrong [good or evil], do not cling to it."

47. It is interesting to note that many of the expressions which Dōgen Zenji uses to describe the attitude or spirit of the tenzo towards his work are identical to several expressions found in the *Fukan Zazen-gi*, in which he describes our attitudes when sitting zazen.

48. *The Regulations of Baizhang* were the first regulations established for running a Zen monastery in China. He lived from A.D. 749 to 814.

49. Uchiyama Rōshi's translation reads: "No matter where we are or whatever circumstances we are in, we are always living out our own life. A fool views his own life as if it were someone else's. Only a wise man realizes that even in his encounters with others, he is living [out] his own life *within* those very encounters."

50. This poem has been attributed to Xuedou.

51. This story of the prodigal son can be found in the Lotus Sutra (*Saddharma-puṇḍarīka-sūtra*) as well as in the Bible.

52. This particular story of Daigui appears in the *Jingde Zhuandeng Lu*, or in Japanese *Keitoku Dentō Roku*, a thirty-section work describing the lineage of the Zen tradition. In the section on Guishan Lingyou (another name for Daigui) we find:

"One day when Daigui was serving as tenzo on Mount Baizhang, he went to wait on the master. Baizhang (Huihai) called out, 'Who is it?' Daigui answered, 'It's me, Lingyou.' Baizhang said, 'Go and stir up the coals. See if any are still burning.' Daigui did as he was told. When he returned, he told Baizhang that the fire was out. Baizhang got up, went to the brazier himself, and raked through the ashes. Finding a small ember still burning way in the back of the brazier he brought it over to Daigui and quipped. 'What do you call this?'

"Daigui suddenly realized what Baizhang had been trying to point out and, after respectfully bowing before his teacher in gratitude, Daigui explained what he had understood. Baizhang responded, 'Your understanding is but a partial deviation from the usual way of understanding.' In the *Nirvāṇa-sūtra* there is a passage which goes: 'If you wish to see buddha-nature, you should contemplate the present cause and circumstances of all things. When the time of enlightenment comes, it is like suddenly clarifying something you had been confused about, like suddenly discovering something you had forgotten. If you reflect on this clearly, there is nothing but yourself. An early patriarch said that gaining enlightenment is the same as before enlightenment. Gain no dharma with no mind.'

"There is no fabrication in reality. Both ordinary men and saints alike are equally living out the incomparable reality of life. Fundamentally, all things lack nothing. You are what you are now. You should take care of this!"

53. Dongshan Shouchu, or in Japanese, Tōzan Shusho, lived around A.D. 807–69. Dongshan's "Three Pounds of Sesame" story appears as the twelfth case of the *Blue Cliff Records*: "A monk asked Dongshan, 'What is buddha?' Dongshan replied, 'Three pounds of sesame' "

54. "Anything of greater value than realization of what the Way," or "any time more precious than the time of realizing the Way." It is very important that the above passage not be taken out of context, and that it is understood on the basis of *mushotoku*, that is, that there is nothing to be gained. Enlightenment is not the sort of thing that becomes some sort of a plus in our life, such as a new car, or some wider knowledge, or relief from physical or mental distress.

In this case, enlightenment should be understood to be completely tied into practice. Uchiyama Rōshi goes into further detail on this point in his commentary on the *Shōbō-genzō: Genjō Kōan*.

55. When, in a previous lifetime, King Asoka was still a child, he was playing with sand one day as Shakyamuni passed by begging alms. The boy offered sand to him as if it were boiled rice, and then bowed. As a result, Shakyamuni foretold that in a future lifetime the boy would become a great king and protector of Buddhism. When Shakyamuni re-

turned home that day he handed the sand over to Ānanda and had him spread it on the path along which Shakyamuni walked during *kinhin*, that is, the intervals of slow walking between periods of zazen.

The above story can be found in the *Ayuwang Jing Zhuyinyuan Pinlue*, or in Japanese, *Aikuō Kyō Shoinnen Bonryaku*.

56. In the *Zuoxaing Yinyuan Jing*, or in Japanese, *Sakuzō Innen Kyō*, there is this story about King Uten: "King Uten approached and asked the Buddha, 'After the death of the Tathagata (Shakyamuni Buddha), I wish to devote my life to carving statues of him. What blessings might be gained from such work?' (Shakyamuni) Buddha replied, 'For generations to come, as your just reward, you would be reborn with a sound body, and upon death you would be reborn into one of the heavenly realms.' "

57. "a spirit of joy and magnanimity, along with the caring attitude of a parent." This is a translation of the Japanese expression *sanshin*, or literally, three minds or attitudes. *Kishin* is a joyful mind; *rōshin* is the mind or attitude of a parent towards a child; while *daishin* is having a magnanimous or "big" mind.

58. Śakro-devānām-indraḥ is one of the two tutelary deities of Buddhism. *Cakravartin* is a technical Sanskrit term meaning literally "one who is characterized by his turning the wheel" or in short, "a wheel-turning monarch." Asoka was so considered. To be able to live and function in a *Saṃgha* community as a tenzo is more favorable than being a king or god (*deva*).

59. "one of the realms of hell, as an insatiable spirit, or as some lowly animal, or as a demon."

Here hell, insatiable spirit, animal, and demon are loose translations for the Sanskrit terms *naraka*, *preta*, *tiryañc*, and *asura*. They refer to various places or forms of rebirth for sentient beings,

and correspond in Japanese to *jigoku, gaki, chikushō*, and *shura*.

In *Farewell to Antai-ji*, Uchiyama Rōshi's final *teishō* (dharma-lecture) before retiring from Antai-ji as abbot, he discussed in some detail the so-called *rokudō zen*, that is, six types of zen.

"It pretty much works out that the depth of one's zazen becomes determined by the attitude with which one sits. The so-called *rokudō zen* has no connection with *shikan-taza*. It is best to stay away from these types of Zen. Let's just look at them for a moment. First of all, *jigoku zen*. You know there are some people who upon just hearing the word zazen get all nervous. This occurs particularly among priests! I'm talking about the kind of priests who are required to live for a certain period of time in an official *sōdō* in order to receive papers which entitle them to be called priests and to take over as head of a temple. They hate being there in the first place, but there's no way to avoid it, and on top of all that, they're forced to do zazen. Doing zazen under those conditions is called *jigoku zen*, or "Zen of hell".

Then there is *gaki zen*. This is the type of Zen done by people who forever go around lusting after enlightenment.

Next comes *chikushō zen*. The word *chikushō* in Japanese refers to an animal that can be domesticated, say a dog or a cat, or maybe a cow. Now in that same sense, there are people who enter a monastery because they hear they'll get fed just by following along. Occasionally, those kinds of people even stray into Antai-ji. They figure that by just being here and sitting in the *sesshin* they will be able to get along. When this kind of person shows up I just have to throw him out. There is an expression "*yoraba taiju no kage.*" It means to look for rest or protection under the shade of a big tree. When people try looking for shade under a scrawny little willow like Antai-ji, though, they're looking for it under the wrong tree. I mean even thinking about being able to eat heartily at Antai-ji—there just aren't any big feeds. The only thing you're likely to get plenty of is brown rice and *miso* soup three times a day. An itinerant priest thinking he will be well taken care of at Antai-ji is really mistaken. That sort of *chikushō zen* is just no good either. People like that ought to be ashamed of themselves.

Following this is *shura zen*. These are the people who compete with others to gain satori. Or else, they vie with one another over whose practice is more severe. Some carry around the *kyōsaku* (stick), beating each other with it. That is *shura zen*.

Then there is *ningen zen*, the Zen that human beings do solely for utilitarian purposes. This is the thing I was talking about previously, that is, people doing zazen to get their heads straightened out or for good health or sexual stamina, and so forth. Anyway, they do zazen in order to gain something from it. There are a lot of books out now on humanistic Zen, or Zen for the body, or Zen and psychology. These are clear examples of *ning enzen*, seeking something beneficial for humanity. In any event, the motive for doing zazen is to get something in return.

Finally we come to *tenjō zen*. These are the people who want to become hermits. There seem to be quite a number of young Americans who like this kind of Zen. It seems as though these young people are trying to run away from the noise of American materialism, so they go up in the mountains to bathe in the quiet relief they find there. Or, when they get bored doing just that, they get caught up in Zen as a hobby and enjoy just polishing the sceptre some priests carry around. Those people are just practicing Zen as a hobby. Naturally, this sort of hermit Zen has nothing to do with the *buddhadharma*. To figure out whether or not you're practicing true zazen or not, you have to look at your practice from as broad a perspective as possible. Once you get stuck in one of these six types of Zen, you are no longer able to see an overall view of the *buddhadharma*.

60. These eight misfortunate conditions or circumstances (*aṣṭākṣaṇāḥ* in Sanskrit), are referred to as the *hachi nanjo* in Japanese. They include being born into one of the many hells depicted in Buddhist literature, or as some insatiable spirit or lowly animal (three of the four mentioned in the above footnote), having good health and abundant wealth, living to an old age, being born before or after the Buddha, being very clever or sophisticated in worldy ways, or being incapacitated due to blindness, deafness, or dumbness.

The first three are the three evil paths of one's past karma; four and five refer to those who are either so healthy or rich or who live to such an old age that they have no feeling for the transiency of life; six refers to the period before and after the death of the Buddha when practicing the dharma is not flourishing, at all; seven refers to people who are too clever and adept in worldly ways; while eight refers to those who are physically handicapped, as the blind, deaf, and dumb.

61. Magnanimous Mind is *daishin*, or literally "big mind" in Japanese. Dōgen Zenji writes of this mind or attitude as being like a mountain or ocean. The mountain is a metaphor for stability or immoveability. That is, one who is swayed neither by enticements nor oppression. The metaphor of the ocean means broadmindedness or tolerance. It is also used to refer to the *saṃgha* community.

62. In a footnote in the *Eihei Daishingi Tsūkai*, edited and compiled by Bun'ei Andō with the collaboration of Shunko Itō and published by Kōmeisha Publishers, there appears the following comment: "The 'sounds of spring' may be seen as words of praise, while the

'fall colors' refers to aspects of things we dislike. One could also think of the 'spring colors' (things we like) and the 'fall sounds' (abuse or criticism)."

63. Jiashan is the name of the mountain or monastery in Hunan Province in southern China. Oftentimes masters who became well-known either within their own lifetime or after their death were referred to by the name of the mountain or monastery in which they resided. Sometimes the name of the mountain is used to indicate where the incident or story took place.

Some sources believe that the tenzo mentioned in the text was Shanhui, a Zen master who established a monastery on Mount Jiashan, although historically this appears impossible. In any case, the following incident between Shanhui and Guishan Lingyou is included 'n Uchiyama Rōshi's footnotes to his commentary to the *Tenzo Kyōkun*. *Jinsei Ryōri no Hon* (How to Cook Your Life).

The following story occured when Shanhui was working as the tenzo on Mount Guishan while Guishan Lingyou was the abbot. One day Guishan approached Shanhui and asked, "What will we be having besides rice today?" Shanhui replied, "The same things we have every spring."

Upon hearing his reply, Guishan encouraged Shanhui to continue his practice. Shanhui responded, "There are dragons residing in the phoenix's nest. [The monks (dragons) here (the phoenix's nest, or the monastery on Mount Jiashan) are practicing very hard.] Guishan thought that here was a monk of real promise.

This account of Shanhui of Jiashan and Guishan appears in the *Chanlin Leiju*, section 18.

64. This account of Daiyuan Fu Shangzuo, or Daigen-fu Jōza in Japanese, appears in volume 17 of the *Wudeng Huiyuan*. Daiyuan Fu lived around the middle of the ninth century.

"One day the great Buddhist scholar Daiyuan Fu was lecturing on the *Mahā-parinirvāṇa-sūtra* at Guangkao-Xiao in Yangzhou when the tenzo of Jiashan who was traveling about from temple to temple (to hear various teachers) happened to stay there for a while due to a heavy snowfall. The tenzo listened to the lecture during which Daiyuan Fu was explaining the section on the three factors of *buddha-nature* and on the three virtues of the *dharmakāya*. In the midst of the scholar's explanation of the subleties of the *dharmakāya*, the tenzo suddenly burst out laughing.

"After the lecture, Daiyuan Fu invited the tenzo to his room and explained, 'Frankly, I am a very simple person and my comments about the sutras which I am lecturing on are very literal. I noticed you broke out laughing when I was talking about the *dharmakāya*. I wonder if you'd be so kind as to tell me where I was in error.'

"The tenzo spoke, 'Well what you said coincides with what is written. In that, you were not in error. It was just that you were talking all around the subject without really knowing it.'

"Shortly after hearing the tenzo's remarks, Daiyuan Fu stopped any further lecturing, and traveled extensively, visiting many masters, inquiring about the *buddhadharma*, and practicing with all his might."

65. This story of Guishan appears in the *Chanlin Leiju*, section 14.

When Guishan Lingyou was living on Mount Baizhang, he went off into the mountains with his teacher, Baizhang Huihai, to work. Baizhang said, "Bring me some fire." Guishan replied, "Okay, I'll bring some right away." When Guishan returned he brought a stick to Baizhang who asked, "Well, where is it?" Guishan proceeded to turn the stick around in his hand, blow on it three times, and hand it to Baizhang. Baizhang took the stick from Guishan, acknowledging the monk's act.

ON THE COMMENTARY

Chapter One

1. Wuzhao, or in Japanese, Mujaku, lived A.D. 820–899.

2. The Wutai mountains, or Godai-zan in Japanese, consist of five main peaks located in the northern part of Shanxi Province, in northern China.

3. This passage was taken from the chapter entitled *Chiji Shingi* of the *Eihei Daishingi* written by Dōgen Zenji in which he carefully establishes a foundation for, and shows through many examples, the deeper significance of having regulations for guiding a community actually gathered together to practice Buddhism.

4. "Hungry ghost" is a literal translation of the Japanese word *gaki*. *Ga* means to be famished or hungry, and *ki* means a demon or ghost. In the context of Zen Buddhism, *gaki* refers to that which arises inside us human beings, and which is never satisfied with what we are or what we have.

5. *Shikan* is a word used to emphasize doing solely whatever word it preceeds, to do only such and such. Here, it carries the additional connotation of doing something wholeheartedly.

6. *Tōji*, which can be written either of two ways in Chinese characters is *samāpatti* or *samādhi* in Sanskrit. The former compound uses the character for "equal" with the character for "hold," meaning to hold or see all things equally, while the latter compound combines the character for "equal" with the character for "approach" or "arrive," meaning to approach all things equally.

7. "Mind and object are innately one" is a traditional translation of the commonly held understanding of the expression *shin ikkyōshō*. Later in the chapter, as Uchiyama Rōshi discusses the expression, he gives the broader interpretation which Dōgen Zenji gave to it. I wish to forewarn the English reader

not to skip over the expression lightly, even though the superficial meaning seems quite obvious.

8. "The buddhadharma should be grasped so that mind and object become one" is a traditional interpretive translation of the expression *shin ikkyō ni hō o sessu*.

9. Again, the commonly held interpretation of the expression *munen musō* implies that the aim of zazen is to try not to think of anything, but of course, that is neither Dōgen Zenji's nor Uchiyama Rōshi's understanding.

The difficulty I face here is to convey the point that when Dōgen Zenji or Uchiyama Rōshi pick up expressions that have been passed down through the ages or comment on non-Buddhist ideas, they are not trying to show why an expression is "wrong," since it is not usually the expression itself which poses a problem. Rather, the emphasis of their approach is to invest a much broader interpretation into the expression.

10. The reader must be very careful in reading this passage, which was taken from volume 5 of the *Eihei Kōroku*. On the surface it appears that Dōgen Zenji is putting down a Buddhist tradition because it differs from Zen. However, that is not the case. What he cautions against is not any particular sect, but rather that a Theravada attitude (similar to the Pharisaic attitude in Judaism?) is to be avoided because it does not see life from the broadest perspective.

11. In Japanese, the expression "mind extends throughout all phenomena, and all phenomena are inseparable from mind" is *isshin issaihō issaihō isshin*.

12. "The most fundamental appearance of things" is a translation of the Japanese expression *honji no fūkō*. Keizan Zenji, in *Zazen Yōjinki* (Points to Watch Concerning Zazen) uses the above term interchangeably with *honrai no menmoku*, often translated as one's "original face."

13. *Jōryo*, literally quiet contemplation, is the Japanese reading of one of

the newer Chinese translations of *dhyāna*.

14. "The deep sky never obstructs the floating white clouds" is the reply Shitou Xiqian gave to Daowu when the latter asked him about the meaning of the *buddhadharma*.

15. *Mokushō zen* expresses the type of zazen practiced in the Sōtō tradition. *Moku* means to sit in silence, while *shō* means to illuminate.

Originally, the expression *mokushō zen* was used as a criticism of the zazen carried on in the Sōtō tradition. Daihui Zonggao called the zazen which Hongzhi Zhengjue and his disciples practiced *mokushō zen*, meaning misdirected Zen in which the practitioner, as an escape from functioning in society, sat reflecting quietly on himself. In other words, Daihui thought it was a king of "navel gazing."

At that time, from the middle of the twelfth century, there was little response to the criticism, although later on Hongzhi Zhengjue wrote a poem entitled *Mokushōmei* in which he used the expression in a very positive way. Traditionally, criticism leveled against the Sōtō tradition is that it becomes narrowly individualistic, a self-illuminating hermitic type of Zen, while criticism often leveled at *kanna zen*, the zazen practiced in the Rinzai tradition, is that it becomes merely a means to gain some sort of satori, or enlightenment experience. The practitioners of both styles must be careful of these dangers.

16. The word "posture" here should be understood to mean both a person's physical posture and also one's mental or emotional posture or attitude.

17. Falling asleep is referred to as *konchin*, while chasing after thoughts is called *sanran*. Sawaki Rōshi used to refer to these states as "sleepy stupor" and "thinking stupor."

18. "practicing single-mindedly with all one's energies" is a translation of the well known Zen expression *isshiki no bendō*. *Isshiki* means to do whatever you are engaged in single-mindedly or wholeheartedly, without becoming distracted. *Bendō* was explained in note 5 accompanying the text of the *Tenzo Kyōkun*.

Chapter Two

1. Nishiari Zenji (1821–1910), whose Buddhist name was Bokusan, was an authority on the *Shōbō-genzō* during the Meiji era. He gave *teishō* (dharma-lectures) on it, the notes of which were compiled, edited, and published under the title of *Shōbō-genzō Keiteki*.

2. The word "tenzo" is used interchangeably, sometimes referring to the office or function of preparing meals and sometimes to the person who performs the work.

3. The Edo period, which is sometimes referred to as the Tokugawa period, extended from about 1603 to 1868.

4. "Teaching beyond letters" is a translation of the expression *furyū monji*. This old Zen expression has become popularly used to imply that in Zen, and therefore, in one's daily life, it is not necessary to use one's mind anymore since Zen is beyond intellect and reason. In other words, the expression has simply become an excuse for some people to sit and vegetate.

Chapter Three

1. "To study the Way of the Buddhas." Refer to note 1 of the *Tenzo Kyōkun*, where Uchiyama Rōshi defines this Japanese expression *butsudō*, or the Way of the Buddhas.

2. Since no human being has ever traveled from one end of the universe to the other end, no one really knows either how large it is, or if what we call the universe might not be simply a part of an even larger entity yet unknown to man.

3. The *Fukan Zazen-gi* (The Way of Zazen for Everyone), was written

by Dōgen Zenji to give us a sort of guideline regarding our physical, mental, or emotional posture when sitting, in addition to advice on our sitting environment. This zazen is universal because it is nonsectarian; it is recommendable because it can be practiced by anyone.

Chapter Four

1. Here, Uchiyama Rōshi is using the word *dōjō* not as a particular building, but rather in the sense that it is used in the *Vimalakīrti-nirdeśa* in the chapter on bodhisattvas in the expression *jikishin kore dōjō*, which means that mind, in the sense of *hṛdaya*, is the place where we practice the Buddha's Way.

Chapter Five

1. These are two similar sounding Japanese words for the similar looking soybean paste (*miso*) and human excrement (*kuso*).

2. Concerning the definition of religion here, Uchiyama Rōshi writes in *Approach to Zen*, "If religion means the teachings about the most refined attitude towards life, then Buddhism is certainly pure religion."

Chapter Six

1. "Three worlds." This is a translation of the expression *sangai*. These worlds consist of the world of desires, both physical and emotional, the world inclusive of forms but without attachment to them, and the world without form or attachment.

2. "Mind and environment are one" derives from the expression *shinkyō ichinyo*. It has the same meaning as the expression *shin ikkyōshō*, mind and object are innately one, that appeared in chapter 1.

3. In the writings of Dōgen Zenji the expression *shikan* is often used interchangeably with the term zazen. For

further details, see *Approach to Zen,* chapter 2.

Shikan-taza has been variously translated as doing "just zazen," "concentrated zazen," or "sitting quietly, doing nothing," although the meaning of "just," "concentrated," or "nothing" is frequently misunderstood. In numerous dharma-lectures, Uchiyama Rōshi often explained it in this way. In Japanese, there are two expressions: *muchū* and *shikan*. Both have the connotation of being engrossed in something, although when the Rōshi used them, the former included a nuance of being carried away by an activity, for example, being caught up in a horse race or football game, while the latter implied being absorbed while at the same time having one's feet on the ground. *Shikan-taza* should be understood in the latter sense and never the former.

4. In a short book entitled *Naki Warai No Takuhatsu* (Laughing Through the Tears), published in the magazine "Mamizu Shinsho" by Hakujusha Publishers, March, 1968, Uchiyama Rōshi takes up several of his experiences during his life of *takuhatsu*, or begging.

Chapter Seven

1. In this case, when the words "good" and "bad" are used, they should not be understood simply in a moralistic way. "Good" in the Buddhist sense means following or living in accordance with the *buddhadharma*. Refer to note 12 of the text of *Tenzo Kyōkun*.

2. "Life" in this case means *shinnyo* or *tathatā*. As the reader can readily understand by now, Uchiyama Rōshi avoids talking about Buddhism by using Buddhist terminology excessively. He has always and vigorously cautioned his disciples and followers to be careful of teachers who are only capable of talking about Buddhism with intricate Buddhist terms. Likewise, he has cautioned against using *his* vocabulary without first

working through it thoroughly in the light of one's own practice.

Chapter Eight

1. The *Shushō-gi* (The Meaning of Practice and Enlightenment) was compiled by Ōuchi Seiran, a lay follower of the Sōtō Zen tradition, and is recognized by the Sōtō Zen School as a guide for laymen and priests. It is made up of passages extracted from the *Shōbō-genzō* which were felt to reflect Dōgen Zenji's most fundamental teachings.

2. *Danken* and *jōken* are two expressions that though both reflecting the absolute nature of life, are at the same time contradictory and one-sided expressions.

Chapter Nine

1. Autumn in Japan is the typhoon season, which not uncommonly ruins entire rice crops. Hence, the farmer pulls weeds in the rice paddy never knowing whether or not he will be able to harvest the crop.

Chapter Ten

1. "Dōgen Zenji's way of practice..." is a translation of *gyōji menmitsu no kafū*. Admittedly, the translation doesn't begin to capture the nuances of the expression. *Gyōji* means the carrying on or maintaining of one's practice, while *menmitsu* comes from another compound *renmen shinmitsu*, which means to carry on something (in this case one's practice) without quitting, and to do it in an intimate or refined or exact manner. *Kafū* refers to a teacher's style or character. In short, then, *gyōji menmitsu no kafū* means constantly and tirelessly refining and deepening one's practice in accord with the character or style of the teacher.

2. *Shogyō mujō*, all things are impermanent, is one of the *sambōin*, that is, three proofs or certifications of the

buddhadharma, the other two being *shohō muga*, nothing has an ego, and *nehan jakujō*, nirvana is quiescence, that is, it is unmoved by our fabricated desires.

3. *Ichinyo* is another expression for *shinjitsu* or *shinnyo* or *tathatā*, that is, undeniable truth. It also implies absolute equality among all things. *Ninyo*, refers to the seeming separation between the Buddha and ourselves.

Chapter Eleven

1. Uchiyama Rōshi did in fact suffer from tuberculosis during his final two years at Antai-ji and for several years after that.

2. Although it was impossible to translate them into English in such a way, it just so happens that in Japanese only six words were used that, coincidentally, all share a common sound with one another.

3. Uchiyama Rōshi relates many of his experiences while on *takuhatsu* and discusses the whys of a life style of begging in chapter 5 of *Godō* (Way Seeker), published by Hakujusha Publishers.

4. The expressions "undeniable truth" and "inescapable reality" are translations of the Japanese expression *zettai shinjitsu*. Although the expression might be better literally translated as "absolute reality," the reader would be misled in understanding how the term is used in the Buddhist sense. "Incomparable reality," not in the superlative sense, but in the sense of being beyond comparison, or rather having no relationship to comparing things, is another way I have translated this expression.

Chapter Twelve

1. A *mondō* is a very brief dialogue of question and reply used widely in Zen Buddhism to talk about the *buddhadharma*.

2. Buddhism first entered Japan prior

to the Nara period through the efforts of Prince Shōtoku around A.D. 600, continuing to enter Japan throughout the Heian period, generally designated as ending around 1185.

Chapter Thirteen

1. "The Self settles naturally upon itself" is another way of expressing the posture of *shikan-taza,* or zazen.

2. An "Etchū *fundoshi*" is the type of loincloth that used to be worn by Japanese men in the province of Etchū, present-day Toyama Prefecture. The pivotal word and humor around which this expression centers is "front." In Japanese, *mae kara,* translated "in front," describes how the loincloth separates, although it carries the meaning of "in the future," where the goals we have set up in our minds, by their very nature, always allude us, since they never coincide with reality.

3. In the *Bendō-wa* (On the Practice of the Way) chapter of the *Shōbō-genzō,* Dōgen Zenji writes: "All the Buddhas and Tathāgatas have an incomparable means for transmitting a mysterious and subtle dharma (life attitude), and for awakening and clarifying one's life. The standard for this transmission, which takes place without error only between Buddhas, is carried on by means of a *samādhi* which functions freely within oneself. That means is the practice of zazen, which is the main entrance into this *samādhi,* enabling one's life to function freely within itself."

4. The expressions *daishin, kishin,* and *rōshin* have been traditionally translated as Big Mind, Joyful Mind, and Parental Mind. Since it is easy to pass them off as psychological states, I have prefered to treat them slightly differently so that the English reader may be able to catch another nuance of the original expression. To understand them as three fundamentally intertwined attitudes toward one's life also follows more closely with the spirit of Uchiyama Rōshi's explanation.

5. "Final refuge" is a translation of the expression *hikkyō kisho.* Literally, the expression means the place to which one ultimately returns.

Chapter Fourteen

1. *Sesshin* are periods of from three days to perhaps two weeks or more when the monastery concentrates more intensely and exclusively on the practice of zazen. Uchiyama Rōshi goes into detail about Antai-ji *sesshin* in his book *Approach to Zen* published by Japan Publications Co.

2. In the city of Kyoto alone, there are over 1,500 shrines and temples, some of which cater to showing several thousand tourists around the grounds each day.

3. In the *Prajñāpāramitā-hṛdaya-sūtra,* commonly known as the *Heart Sutra,* there is this phrase: *fuzō fugen fuku fujō,* or "no increase, no decrease, no purity, no impurity," from which the above quotation was taken.

Glossary

Abbreviations used: Skt. (Sanskrit), Ch. (Chinese Pinyin),
W. (Wade-Giles), J. (Japanese)

Ayuwang Jing W., *A-yü-wang Ching;* J., *Aikuo-kyō. The Sutra of King Asoka.*
Ayuwang Jing Zhuyinyuan Pinlue W., *A-yü-wang Ching Chu-yin-yüan P'in-lueh;*
J., *Aikuo-kyō Shoinnen Bonryaku.* Contains the story about King Uten
and Shakyamuni Buddha.
Awakening of bodhisattva spirit See *hotsu bodaishin.*

Baizhang Qinggui W., *Pai-chang Ch'in-kuei;* J., *Hyakujō Shingi.* An eight
section volume dealing with the regulations in a Zen monastery written
by Baizhang Huihai (q.v.) around the late eighth and early ninth centuries.
Baizhang Huihai W., Pai-chang Hui-hai; J., Hyakujō Ekai. Lived
749–814.
Baoneng Renyong W., Pao-neng Jen-yung; J., Honei Ninyu. Died
1049.
bodhi Ch., *pudi;* W., *p'u-ti;* J., *bodai.* The wisdom of enlightenment,
acquired through the cutting off of all passions and illusions.
bodhicitta Ch., *pudixin;* W., *p'u-ti hsin;* J., *bodaishin.* Awakening mind
or spirit. That is, a mind or attitude which faces in the direction of buddha.
An attitude which settles upon the reality of life. See also *dōshin.*
bodhisattva Ch., *pusa;* W., *p'usa;* J., *bosatsu.* An ordinary human
being who takes up a course in life that moves in the direction of buddha.
See Buddha.
bodhi-spirit See *bodhicitta.*
body of Buddha Ch., *foshen;* W., *fo-shen;* J., *busshin;* Skt., *buddhakāya.*
An expression for the limitless powers of the Buddha-nature.
Buddha Ch. & W., *fo;* J., *butsu* or *hotoke.* Sometimes refers to Shakyamuni Buddha, although often (usually lower case) extends to include
all those who have awakened to the reality of life. One of the Three
Treasures (q.v.).

buddhadharma Ch., *fofa;* W., *fo-fa;* J., *buppō.* Refers specifically to the teachings of Shakyamuni, but most broadly to the reality of life as it is when experienced from the viewpoint of *satori* (q.v.).

butsuden Ch., *fodian;* W., *fo-tien.* One of the buildings or large halls in which a statue of a buddha or bodhisattva is enshrined. Refer to note 29 of the *Tenzo Kyōkun.*

butsudō Ch., *fodao;* W., *fo-tao;* Skt., *buddhamārga.* Sometimes refers to the Buddha's teachings and sometimes to the path (Skt., *mārga*) or practice leading to or embodying enlightenment. *Dō* was originally the translation of the Sanskrit word *bodhi.* The later expression *bodhicitta* was originally *dōshin,* meaning enlightened mind. *Dō* in the sense of path can be found in such expressions as *hasshō-dō,* the eightfold path.

butsuji Ch., *foshi;* W., *fo-shih;* Skt., *buddhakārya.* Those activities that accord with buddha, or the true reality of life.

byakugōkō Ch., *baihaoguang;* W., *pai-hao kuang;* Skt., *urnakeśa.* A ray of light emitted from the Buddha's third eye whenever he spoke on *buddhadharma.*

Chanyuan Qinggui W., *Ch'an-yüan Ch'ing-kuei;* J., *Zen'en Shingi.* A ten-section work regarding the regulations for running a monastery. Written by Zongze of Mount Zhanglu (J., Chōro Sōsaku), in 1103.

citta Ch., *xin;* W., *hsin;* J., *shin* or *kokoro.* In the narrowest sense *citta* refers to the psychological (mental or emotional) mind, although in the *Tenzo Kyōkun* it is almost always used in the broader sense of *hrdaya* (q.v.).

daishin Ch., *daxin;* W., *ta-hsin.* Literally, *daishin* means Big (or magnanimous) Mind. One of the "three minds," the other two being Parental Mind and Joyful Mind.

Daiyuan Fu W., Tai-yüan Fu; J., Daigen Fu. Dates unknown.

danken Ch., *duanjian;* W., *tuan-chien;* Skt., *ucchedadrsti.* A view of life which holds that upon the death of the individual nothing will survive. A doctrine of annihilation as opposed to an eternalistic view. See also *jōken.*

Deshan Yijian W., Te-shan Yi-chien; J., Tokusan Senkan. Lived 780–865. Noted for his brusk teaching style.

dharma Ch. & W., *fa;* J., *hō.* Dharma has four basic meanings. The first is *hetu,* that is, seed or cause, which, through the correct relationship of cause and effect, points to truth. Second is *guna* or ethical virtue. Third is *śāsana,* the Buddha's teachings and the fourth is *prakrti,* the essence of all phenomena.

dōjō Ch., *daochang;* W., *tao-ch'ang;* Skt., *bodhimanda.* Narrowly speaking, *dōjō* designates the place where Buddhists can practice, that is, the actual buildings and grounds. Broadly speaking, however, it includes whatever situations or circumstances in which people practice the Buddha's way of life. This is the deeper sense of the expression *jiki shin kore dōjō,* mind as it is, is the place for practice.

Dongshan Liangjie W., Tung-shan Liang-chieh; J., Tōzan Ryōkai. Died 869.

Dongshan Shouchu W., Tung-shan Shou-ch'u; J., Tōzan Shusho. Died 990.

dōshin Ch., *daoxin;* W., *tao-hsin;* Skt., *bodhicitta.* The mind which aspires and endeavors to realize perfect enlightenment. The aspiration to deepen and refine one's life. See also *bodhicitta.*

Eihei Daishingi A five-chapter volume dealing with the regulations for running a monastery. Written by Dōgen Zenji over a period of twelve years (1237–49).

Eihei Daishingi Tsūkai A one volume work containing the original *kambun* (Japanese written in Chinese style) text along with a modern Japanese version and commentary. The Japanese "translation" and commentary were written by Andō Bun'ei with the collaboration of Itō Shunkō, and published by Komeisha Press, Tokyo, 1936.

Eihei Kōroku The full title is *Eihei Dōgen Oshō Kōroku.* This work contains various statements made by Dōgen Zenji over a period of many years. It was compiled by a number of Dōgen's disciples shortly after his death.

Eihei Shingi See *Eihei Daishingi.*

Fukan Zazen-gi Written by Dōgen Zenji around 1228 while he was residing at Kennin-ji in Kyoto. It contains a very concise explanation of zazen as the main gate to enter in practicing the Buddha's way of life.

Furong Daokai W., Fu-jung Tao-k'ai; J., Fuyō Dōkai. Lived 1043–1118.

Fushan Fayuan W., Fu-shan Fa-yüan; J., Fuzan Hōen. Lived 991–1067.

fūsu Ch., *fusi;* W., *fu-ssu.* One of the six *chiji,* or head priests, of the monastery. The *fusu* is specifically in charge of financial and clerical affairs.

Gakudō Yōjinshū A short treatise dealing with the major points of Buddhist practice. The *Gakudō Yōjinshū* was completed by Dōgen Zenji while he was residing at Kōshō-ji, at that time located in Fukakusa on the outskirts of Kyoto, in 1234.

gāthā Ch., *song;* W., *sung;* J., *ju.* Verses extolling the *buddhadharma.* In Zen, *gāthā* are used to express succinctly the essence hidden in the koans.

Genjō Kōan Depending upon the version, it is the first or third chapter of the *Shōbō-genzō* of Dōgen Zenji. It was written around 1233. In the *Genjō Kōan,* Dōgen totally redefines koan (q.v.) as being a direct manifestation of reality itself rather than a device used to gain insight.

genuine Zen See *ichimi zen.*

gomi zen See *ichimi zen.*

Guishan Lingyou W., Kuei-shan Ling-yu; J., Isan Reiyū. Lived 770–853.

Hongzhi Zhenghue   W., Hung-chih Chen-chüo;   J., Wanshi Shōgaku. Lived 1091–1157.

hotsu bodaishin, or *hosshin*   An attitude which aspires to buddhahood through the four bodhisattva vows (to save all sentient beings, to extinguish the passions, to study all teachings, and to attain the Buddha-truth) and the practice of the six paramitas (giving, keeping the precepts, perseverance, assiduity, meditation, and wisdom). The turning of one's spirit away from egocentricity towards the reality of life.

hṛdaya   Ch., *xin;*   W., *hsin;*   J., *shin* or *kokoro.* The buddha-mind (cf. *bodhicitta*); also used to indicate the buddha-nature, or potential for buddhahood, inherent in all things (Skt., *tathāgatagarbha*). See also *citta.*

ichimi zen   Ch., *yiweichan;*   W., *yi-wei ch'an.* Unadulterated Zen; the Zen of the buddhas and patriarchs. Literally, *ichimi* means one taste or flavor; the compound implies nondiscrimination or equality. As opposed to *gomi zen* (variously-tainted Zen), that is, Zen practiced for some ulterior motive.

ichinyo   Ch., *yiru;*   W., *yi-ju;*   Skt., *tathatā.* An expression of the individuality of the reality of life. *Ichi,* one, means incomparable, that is, beyond comparison. *Nyo* means as something actually is. Therefore, the Truth of life as it is, prior to human discrimination.

ino   Ch., *weina;*   W., *wei-na.* One of the six *chiji,* or head priests, of the monastery. The *ino* is responsible for the personal affairs within the temple.

isshin issaihō issaihō isshin   Ch., *yixin yiqiefa yiqiefa yixin;*   W., *yi-hsin yi-ch'ieh-fa yi-ch'ieh-fa yi-hsin.* Mind extends throughout or permeates all phenomena, and all phenomena are inseparable from mind. This expression can be found in both the *Shōbō-genzō: Sokushin-zebutsu* and the *Shōbō-genzō: Tsuki.*

Jiashan Shanhui   W., Chia-shan Shan-hui;   J., Kassan Zen'e. Lived 805–81.

Jianyuan Zhongxing   W., Chian-yüan Chung-hsing;   J., Zengen Chūkō. Dates unknown, but probably spanned late eighth and early ninth centuries.

Jijuyū-zammai   A treatise written by Menzan Zuihō (1683–1769) and first published in 1738. It is not a commentary on the *Jijuyū-zammai* section of Dōgen Zenji's *Shōbō-genzō: Bendō-wa,* but rather Menzan's own understanding of *jijuyū-zammai* (q.v.).

jijuyū-zammai   The freedom to accept and give life to everything that one encounters in one's life.

Jingde Zhuandeng Lu   W., *Ching-te Chuan-teng Lu;*   J., *Keitoku Dentō-roku.* A thirty-chapter work compiled by Daoxuan (J., Eian Dōgen) in China in the eleventh century. A who's who of the Zen lineage beginning from the seven Buddhas prior to Shakyamuni down through Fayan Wenyi (J., Hōgen Moneki; lived 885–958; founder of a school of Zen).

jiriki   Ch., *zili;*   W., *tzu-li. Self-power,* or the power derived from personal intelligence and discrimination. *Jiriki* is often used to indicate an individual's attempt to gain enlightenment through his own efforts rather than through relying on the power or compassion of the Buddha. *Jiriki* is contrasted with *tariki* or *other-power*. Although it is often said that Pure Land Buddhism is *tariki* and Zen is *jiriki*, in fact, neither is one or the other.

jōken Ch., *changjian;* W., *ch'ang-chien;* Skt., *śāsvata-dṛṣṭi*. Sometimes referred to as *uken*. A view of life that sees the world as unchanging and continuing even after one's death. Opposite of *danken* (q.v.).

jōrokushin Abbreviation of *jōroku-konjin*. Literally, it means a golden body that stands sixteen feet tall; thus, an epithet for Shakyamuni Buddha.

jōryo Ch., *jinglu;* W., *ching-lu*. Quiet contemplation. From one of the later Chinese translations of the Sanskrit word *dhyāna*. See also *samādhi*.

jōshin Ch., *chengxin;* W., *cheng-hsin*. True sincerity or wholeheartedness.

Joyful Mind See *kishin*.

kamado A wood-burning stove made of adobe, stone, or brick, and used for cooking in both China and Japan. There are still a few monasteries in Japan that use a *kamado* for cooking.

kansu Ch., *jiansi;* W., *chien-su*. One of the six *chiji*, or head priests, in the monastery. The *kansu* is in charge of the overall affairs in the temple.

Keitoku Dentō-roku See *Jingde Zhuandeng Lu*.

kenshō Ch., *jianxing;* W., *chien-hsing*. An insight into the nature of self. The word is used very little by Dōgen, and then, only negatively. The reason for this is that for Dōgen true enlightenment is not a matter of some provisional, temporary insight on the part of a human being after which practice is no longer necessary. Dōgen taught that enlightenment cannot be separated from practice, and that human insight, at best, is just the parabolic touching of the elephant by a blind man.

kesa Ch., *jiasha;* W., *chia-sha;* Skt., *kaśāya*. An outer robe worn by a priest over his other robes. In Japan and China one way the *kesa* is worn is over the left shoulder and under the right one; it is a robe which indicates that one is a follower of Shakyamuni Buddha. Due to differences in climate between India and China, the *kesa* is sometimes worn differently in China.

Kie Buppōsō-hō The eighty-eighth chapter of the *Shōbō-genzō* of Dōgen Zenji which deals with the virtues of having faith in the Three Treasures (the Buddha, the Saṃgha, and the Dharma).

kishin Ch., *xixin;* W., *hsi-hsin*. One of the "three minds"; the other two being *rōshin* and *daishin* (q.v.). *Kishin* means Joyful Mind, that is, having a spirit of joyfulness, regardless of the task.

koan Ch., *gongan;* W., *kung-an*. A word originally meaning a public notice or statement issued by the government. In Zen, however, it refers to the stories and comments made by various teachers in the past and used as themes for meditation by Zen students. The koans usually reflect a particular universal truth. Although Dōgen Zenji was familiar with the koans, and in fact, collected 300 of the most important ones, his attitude towards them can be seen through the title of one of the chapters of the *Shōbō-genzō* entitled *Genjō Kōan*, in which Dōgen changes the meaning of koan from some problem on which the student meditates while doing zazen, to whatever is before us to which we have to open our eyes and deal with. In other words, all of our day-to-day activities as well as the overall direction of our lives are our koan.

kusu Ch., *kusu;* W., *k'u-ssu*. Originally, the *kusu* was the priest in charge of the overall affairs of the monastery. In the *Chanyuan Qinggui* (q.v.) the *kusu* is synonomous with *kan'in*, or superior. Later *kusu* became the general name for the three *chiji*, or head priests, called *ino, tsūsu*, and *kansu* (q.v.).

Linji Lu W., *Lin-chi Lu;* J., *Rinzai-roku*. A one-volume work compiled by a later disciple of Linji Yixuan (J., Rinzai Gigen, died 867; founder of Rinzai school).

Magnanimous Mind See *daishin*.

mantoku enman Ch., *wande yuanman;* W., *wan-te yüan-man. Mantoku* means doing many virtuous deeds, while *enman* is an expression which means complete or perfect; hence, a person of perfected virtues, is said to be *enman*. Thus, *mantoku enman* describes one who demonstrates his character through taking meticulous care of all those around him.

mind See *citta*.

mokushō zen Ch., *mozhao chan;* W., *mo-chao ch'an*. An expression for the type of zazen practiced in the Sōtō tradition. Originally, the term was used derogatorily to describe the zazen of Hongzhi Zhengjue (J., Wanshi Shōgaku; lived 1091–1157). *See* note 15, chapter 1 for more details.

monastery See *saṃgha*.

mondō Ch., *wenda;* W., *wen-ta*. Question and reply, especially between a teacher and a disciple.

munen musō Ch., *wunian wuxiang;* W., *wu-nien wu-hsiang*. No notion, no thought. That is, the aim of zazen envisioned as a stage where discriminative thought does not arise. This is a mistaken understanding of the sixth Patriarch's expression.

Myōzen Butsuju Lived 1184–1225. A priest of the Rinzai School. Born in Mie Prefecture and studied on Mount Hiei and at Kennin-ji in Kyoto under Eisai Zenji. He went to China with Dōgen Zenji and died there.

nehan jakujō See *sambō-in*.

ninyo Ch., *erru;* W., *er-ju*. The seeming separation between Buddha and ourselves.

Parental Mind See *rōshin*.

Qingyuan Xingsi W., Ch'ing-yüan Hsing-ssu; J., Seigen Gyōshi. Exact dates unknown; however, Qingyuan was a disciple of the sixth patriarch, Huineng (J., Eno) who lived during the late seventh and early eighth centuries.

Rinzai-roku See *Linji Lu.*

rōshi Ch. *laoshi;* W., *lao-shih* A Zen master or teacher of the lineage regarded as enlightened.

rōshin Ch., *laoxin;* W., *lao-hsin.* One of the "three minds." The other two are *daishin* and *kishin* (q.v.). Rōshin refers to having the mind of a parent or true adult.

ryōri Ch., *liaoli;* W., *liao-li.* Originally, *ryōri* meant to calculate and manage things. In a deeper sense it refers to the overall management or conduct of our day-to-day life. Later on, the use of the word became more specialized and came to mean the management and cooking of food. In this book it is used in both ways, although its original sense is being emphasized.

samādhi Ch., sanwei; W., san-wei; J., sammai. Narrowly translated as concentrated meditation. Sawaki Kōdō Rōshi defined *samādhi* as "doing self with self by self". In other words, there is nothing outside of Self. Self, here, should not be misunderstood to mean the individual self, but the Self as a whole going beyond skin and bones, mind and emotions. Seeing and carrying out all of one's activities as if *everything* were a *part* of one's body is *samādhi.* See also *tōji.*

samāpatti See *tōji.*

sambō *See* Three Treasures.

sambō-in Ch., *sanfayin;* W., *san-fa yin.* The three distinguishing marks which set Buddhism apart from non-Buddhist religions. The first is *shogyō mujō,* all things are impermanent; the second is *shohō muga,* all things are unsubstantial and have no permanent selfness; and the third is *nehan jakujō,* nirvana is quiescence (all things as they are before delusion). Since all things are impermanent and without a substantial self, it follows that there can be no decay.

samgha Ch., *conglin;* W., *ts'ung-lin;* J., *sōrin* or *sōdan.* A community of monks or lay practitioners gathered together for the common purpose of practicing zazen. Usually a *samgha* consists of a minimum of three or four people.

sammai See *samādhi.*

satori Ch. & W., *wu.* Enlightenment; awakening. Usually understood as the opposite of delusion (J., *mayoi;* Skt., *māyā*). More deeply it is an awakening beyond enlightenment or delusion.

seisei Ch., *jingcheng;* W., *ching-ch'eng.* (Sometimes read as *shōjō* in Japanese.) Used to describe the attitude of absolute sincerity that any practitioner should have towards his everyday activities. It is also an attitude which meets everything we encounter in our lives with sincerity and a straightforward spirit. Sometimes used in contrast to the word *zenna* (q.v.). See also *shōjō; zōzen.*

sesshin Ch., *shexin;* W., *she-hsin.* In most monasteries in Japan *sesshin* are three, five, or seven day periods in which the residents in the monastery gather together for zazen. The number of days and periods of sitting during any one day vary with the monastery. For further information on *sesshin* refer to Uchiyama Roshi's *Approach to Zen.*

shikan   Ch., *zhiguan;* W., *chih-kuan.* Just or only. (It should not be confused with the *shikan* of the Tendai School meaning *śamatha-vipaśyanā,* to give up illusions and attain enlightenment.)

shikan-taza   Ch., *zhiguan dazuo;* W., *chih-kuan ta-tso.* Just doing zazen. Sometimes it is referred to as "themeless sitting," since practitioners of *shikan-taza* simply concentrate on sitting without meditating on an object, koan, or any other artificial device.

shin   See *citta.*

shin ikkyōshō   Ch., *xin yijingxing;* W., *hsin yi-ching hsing.* Mind and object (or environment) are inseparable. It is also another name for *samādhi* (q.v.).

shishin   Ch., *zhixin;* W., *chih-hsin;* Skt., *apratiṣṭhita-citta.* Abbreviation of *shōjōshin,* or pure mind. That is, functioning in our day-to-day activities without ulterior motives.

shissui   Ch., *zhisui;* W., *chih-sui.* One of the six *chiji,* or head priests. The *shissui* is in charge of the maintainance of both the buildings and grounds and the work schedule in the monastery.

Shōbō-genzō   A ninty-five chapter work of Dōgen Zenji composed after he returned from China (at age thirty-two) until his death at fifty-four. As an expression it could be translated as being the essence of the highest teachings of the Buddha, or the essence of the reality of life.

shōgon jōshin   Ch., *jingqin chengxin;* W., *ching-ch'in ch'eng-hsin;* Practicing with a pure mind and willingness to make effort all day and all night as the need calls for.

shogyō mujō   See *sambō-in.*

shohō muga   See *sambō-in.*

shōji   Ch. *shengsi;* W., *sheng-ssu;* Skt., *saṃsāra.* Birth (or life) and death. *Shōji* is the name of one of the chapters of the *Shōbō-genzō* of Dōgen Zenji.

shōjō   Ch., *gingjing;* W., *ch'ing-ching;* Skt., *vyavadāna; viśuddha.* Purification of illusion. Used in contrast to *zōzen* (q.v.). See also *seisei; zenna.*

shuryō   Ch., *zhongliao;* W., *chung-liao.* One of the buildings in a monastery. Differing from the *sōdō,* in which the monks practice zazen, the *shuryō* is more for studying and having tea in a formal situation, or taking the evening meal. Not all monasteries have both.

Shushōgi   The full title is *Sōtō-shū Kyōkai Shushōgi.* It consists of five chapters and was compiled from excerpts taken from various chapters of the *Shōbō-genzō* during mid-Meiji era, around 1890.

sōdō   Ch., *sengtang;* W., *sen-t'ang.* The central building of the monastery in which the monks gather for zazen, meals, and sleeping.

Soeishū   Ch., *Zuyingji;* W., *Tsu-ying Chi.* A twenty-chapter work written by Xuedou Zhongxian (J., Setchō Juken).

sokushin-zebutsu   Ch., *jixin zhefo;* W., *chi-hsin che-fo.* While "mind" is just ordinary, it is at the same time buddha. That is, *mind,* just as it is, is *buddha.*

sōtō   Ch., *Caodong;*   W., *Ts'ao-tung.* The Sōtō school of Zen; an abbreviation of the names of the first two Chinese patriarchs of this school.

Suttanipāta   One of the oldest Buddhist scriptures said to include direct oral statements made by Shakyamuni Buddha.

takuhatsu   Ch., *tuobo;*   W., *t'o-po;*   Skt., *piṇḍapātika.* Mendicant begging.

teishō   Ch., *dichang;*   W., *ti-ch'ang.* Dharma-lectures, or explanations about the Buddhist teachings.

tenzo   Ch., *dianzuo;*   W., *tien-tso.* One of the six *chiji*, or head priests. The *tenzo* is responsible for the management and cooking of all food in the monastery.

Tenzo Kyōkun   The first chapter of Dōgen Zenji's *Eiheigen Zenji Shingi* (Regulations for the Monastery), here translated as *Instructions for the Zen Cook.*

three minds   See *daishin, kishin,* and *rōshin.*

Three Treasures   Ch., *sanbao;*   W., *san-pao;*   Skt., *ratna-traya;*   J., *sambō.* The Buddha, the Dharma, and the Saṃgha, the three most precious elements in Buddhism.

tōji   Ch., *dengzhi;*   W., *teng-chih;*   Skt., *samāpatti.* One of the seven names of *samādhi.*

tōji   Ch., *dengchi;*   W., *teng-ch'ih;*   Skt., *samādhi.* See *samādhi.* (Coincidentally, the Chinese translations for *samāpatti* and *samādhi* sound the same in Japanese, even though they are written with different characters.)

tsūsu   Ch., *dousi;*   W., *tou-su.* Originally, the *tsūsu* was the head of the affairs of the monastery, but as the monasteries in China grew, the work was divided between three officers; the *tsūsu, kansu,* and *fūsu* (q.v.).

wisdom   See *bodhi, bodhicitta.*

Wudeng Huiyuan   W., *Wu-teng Hui-yüan;*   J., *Gotō Egen.* Contains the story of Daiyuan Fu and the tenzo from Jiashan.

Wuzhao Wenxi   W., Wu-chao Wen-hsi;   J., Mujaku Bunki, Lived 820–99.

Xuedou Zhongxian   W., Hsüeh-tou Chung-hsien;   J., Setchō Juken. Lived 980–1052.

Xuefeng Yicun   W., Hsüeh-feng Yi-ts'un;   J., Seppō Gison. Lived 821–908.

Yangshan Huiji   W., Yang-shan Hui-chi;   J., Gyōzan Ejaku. Lived 807–83.

Yuanwu Keqin   W., Yüan-wu K'e-ch'in;   J., Engo Kokugon. Lived 1063–1135.

yuiga dokuson   There is a legend which says that when Shakyamuni Buddha was born he said, "I alone am revered in heaven and earth." In this case, of course, "I" means "Self" in its broadest sense.

Yuibutsu Yōbutsu One of the later chapters of the *Shōbō-genzō.* Only buddha recognizes buddha.

zagu Ch., *zuoju;* W., *tso-chü;* Skt., *niṣīdana.* A square piece of cloth spread out on the ground or floor. The priest either sits on top of or does prostrations on the *zagu,* depending upon what the situation calls for. Its original purpose was to keep the *kesa* (q.v.) from touching the ground or floor.

zazen Ch., *zuochan;* W., *tso-ch'an.* Literally, seated meditation. In the *Tenzo Kyōkun* it also refers to living our lives with the attitude of a buddha.

Zen Ch., *chan;* W., *ch'an;* Skt., *dhyāna.* In Bendō-wa of the *Shōbō-genzō* Dōgen Zenji explains that the word *chan* in China was an abbreviation of *zuochan,* or zazen, and that the expression *zenshū,* or Zen school, arose out of the ignorance of people who did not understand that zazen itself is the practice of the *buddhadharma* (q.v.).

zenna Ch., *ranwu;* W., *jan-wu;* Skt., *kliṣṭa.* Defiled; a term denoting deeds (both good and evil) barring one from enlightenment. Used in contrast to *seisei* (q.v.). See also *Shōjō; zōzen.*

Zen'en Shingi See *Chanyuan Qinggui.*

Zhanglu Zongze W., Chuang-lu Tsung-tse; J., Chōro Sōsaku. Dates unknown, but thought to have lived around the twelfth century. Famous for his *Zazen-gi* and other writings.

zōzen Ch., *zaran;* W., *tsa-jan;* Skt., *saṃkleśa.* Literally, various impurities. The defilement of illusion, resulting from good, evil, and neutral actions. Used in contrast to *shōjō* (q.v.). See also *seisei: zenna.*

Zuimonki The *Shōbō-genzō Zuimonki.* Various statements about Buddhism and Buddhist practice made by Dōgen Zenji and compiled by his chief disciple Kōun Ejō. The most important themes which come up again and again in various sections of the five chapters deal with the casting off of egocentric thoughts and actions, the importance of living in poverty, and the practice of zazen.

 The "weathermark" identifies this book as a production of John Weatherhill, Inc., publishers of fine books on Asia and the Pacific. Book design and typography by Miriam F. Yamaguchi and Stephen B. Comee. Composition by Korea Textbook, Seoul. Printing by Shōbundō, Tokyo. Binding by Okamoto, Tokyo. The typeface used is Monotype Baskerville.